| DATE DUE | | | |
|---|---|---|---|
| | | | |
| | | | |
| | | | |
| | | | |
| | | | |
| | | | |
| | | | |
| | | | |
| | | | |
| | | | |
| | | | |
| | | | |

# Afro-American Fiction, 1853-1976

# Afro-American Fiction, 1853-1976

## A GUIDE TO INFORMATION SOURCES

*Volume 25 in the American Literature, English
Literature, and World Literatures in English
Information Guide Series*

### Edward Margolies

*Professor of American Literature and American Studies
College of Staten Island
City University of New York*

### David Bakish

*Assistant Professor of English
Medgar Evers College
City University of New York*

*Gale Research Company*
Book Tower, Detroit, Michigan 48226

To Our Parents,

Bessie Margolies
and
Rose and Marco Bakish

# VITAE

Edward Margolies is a professor of American literature and American studies at the College of Staten Island, City University of New York. He received his B.A. in English from Brown University, M.A. in English from New York University, and Ph.D. in American studies from New York University, in 1964.

Margolies is the author of NATIVE SONS; A CRITICAL STUDY OF TWENTIETH-CENTURY NEGRO AMERICAN AUTHORS (Lippincott, 1968) and THE ART OF RICHARD WRIGHT (Southern Illinois University Press, 1969). He has also contributed many articles in the Afro-American studies and literature fields.

David Bakish is an assistant professor of English at Medgar Evers College, City University of New York. He received his B.A. and M.A. in English from Bucknell University, and Ph.D. in English from the University of Delaware, in 1971.

Bakish is the author of RICHARD WRIGHT (Ungar, 1973), and he has contributed to the periodical, STUDIES IN BLACK LITERATURE, and the ENCYCLOPEDIA OF WORLD LITERATURE IN THE 20TH CENTURY.

# CONTENTS

# ACKNOWLEDGMENTS

Although we are, of course, responsible for the contents of this work, the following persons have been extremely helpful in our research: Robert A. Bone, Teachers College, Columbia University; Robert A. Corrigan, University of Maryland; Ernest Kaiser, Schomburg Collection of Negro Literature, New York Public Library; Ann Allen Shockley, Fisk University Library; Mary Fair Burks, University of Maryland, Eastern Shore; Theodore Grieder, Fales Collection, New York University. We are especially grateful to William French, University Place Book Shop, New York City, for checking our manuscript and providing us with important biographical and bibliographical information.

# INTRODUCTION

Strictly speaking, Afro-American fiction may well have begun before 1853. Robert Bone cites the possibility of two or three earlier tales, but regardless of origins, Afro-American fiction was influenced largely by the principal literary activity of Negroes up until this time--slave narratives.[1] These were, in the main, brief autobiographical accounts of former slaves telling of their lives under bondage and of their subsequent experiences in the North. From the 1840s on they were most often published by abolitionist societies, and although they were intended as propaganda, many were not without literary value. So widespread was their readership that they probably helped engender the counter literary propaganda of the plantation novel.

These narratives were curious documents because they frequently directed themselves to two different audiences--black and white--and as a result, the messages they contain are rather mixed, if not contradictory. As many Afro-American authors themselves remark, the question of audience has long plagued blacks, and has been compounded by the fact that most major publishers are white and their readerships white. When these publishers think it advisable to print the works of black authors, they anticipate images of black life that accord with the prevailing cultural stereotypes--anything from the obsequious darky of the 1880s to the raging militant of the 1960s. Only the rare white publisher has recognized or encouraged artistic independence in black writers. As a consequence many Afro-American authors have from the start subsidized their own works (and still do), aiming for audiences, black and white, who they hope will not prejudge their case.

What the slave narratives bequeathed to subsequent generations of black authors are the following: perceptions of Negro "lowlife" and folklore; an emphasis on religiosity, especially Christianity as a supportive element of the slaves' existence under duress; nascent elements of militancy and race pride as the slaves attempt to resist oppressive masters; the theme of flight; the celebration of freedom; and a stress on courage, resourcefulness, perseverance and frugality as means of survival and even success. In odd ways these narratives were indeed success stories intended to inspire black readers ("How I rose from the status of a slave to that of a free man or my development from a slave's consciousness to a free consciousness."), as well as to arouse white readers to the injustices of racism. Often their works were pedantic and digressive, stopping to explain something to black or white readers that one or the other might not know. Finally, and not surprisingly, the autobiographical voices of these narrators are often transferred to works of fiction--so much so, that the bibliographer is occasionally at a loss to determine whether a book is autobiographical fiction or fictional autobiography.[2]

Of course, not all of the elements of the slave narrative are to be found in every work of fiction from 1853 to the present. Depending upon the period in which a work is written (not to mention the particular genius of an artist), some elements are stressed, some neglected, and some may be regarded as latent. For purposes of this essay we shall divide Afro-American writing into blocks of time in accordance with what we believe are some of its major themes. It must not be supposed, however, that because some themes are dominant, others do not exist. For example, the years 1890-1915 can hardly be called a period of nationalism and militancy even though nationalist and militant elements may be found in some of the novels of Sutton Griggs and W.E.B. DuBois.

As any cursory glance at this bibliography will indicate, the works of fiction between William Wells Brown's CLOTEL (1853), Frank J. Webb's THE GARIES AND THEIR FRIENDS (1857), and the novels and short stories of the 1890s are few and far between. Yet each of these early novels foreshadows, in its own way, that first full flowering of Negro letters which would extend until roughly 1915. CLOTEL, which was in some respects close to the slave narrative form, tells of the escape and melodramatic adventures of a half-white slave girl. Although its literary value is not worth pondering, it does focus on the ironies of social injustice and the dilemmas of persons of mixed blood. THE GARIES, on the other hand, deals far less with racial prejudice and far more with the solid bourgeois qualities of the protagonist and his circle. In the 1890-1915 period, the kind of material Brown and Webb have dealt with would become major preoccupations of Afro-American writers.

Perhaps the novel that best exemplifies this is James Weldon Johnson's AUTO-BIOGRAPHY OF AN EX-COLORED MAN (1911), whose cultured, educated, and light-skinned protagonist is constantly thwarted in his attempts to become a serious composer because of race, and in the end he passes himself off as white. An interesting aspect of this work is Johnson's informative but condescending treatment of working-class Negroes. This tone of class superiority may also be found in some of the novels of Charles Waddell Chesnutt and Paul Laurence Dunbar. But in Chesnutt's short fiction, CONJURE WOMAN TALES (1899), the shambling, seemingly ineffectual Uncle Julius, who tells "quaint" but quietly devastating stories about old plantation days, often outwits or manipulates his patronizing white interrogator. The respect Chesnutt proffers Uncle Julius is occasionally matched by Paul Laurence Dunbar's portrayal of Southern Negro peasants (although for the most part they appear as funny dialect-speaking darkies). However, it would not be until the so-called Negro Renaissance period, 1915-33, that black writers would celebrate the poor, the "ordinary," and the marginal as the salt of the earth.

The Renaissance coincided with the rising expectations of Negroes as they moved north to cities and the hopes of equality engendered by the rhetoric of World

War I. When these lay shattered by economic recession and racial tensions, black reactions ranged from race pride and cultural and political nationalism to a kind of retreat into the image of the Negro as noble savage--someone apart from and superior to a corrupt and neurotic white civilization. In certain respects, of course, nationalism and primitivism of this sort had their counterparts beyond the Negro community in budding anti-imperialist movements, the advent of communism in Russia which encouraged such movements, and a renewed interest in the "primitive" arts of Asia and Africa. In America the vogue of Freud and an awakening interest in jazz fueled a new curiosity about blacks that was both exploited and publicized by the white writer, Carl Van Vechten. The Negro Renaissance (sometimes called the Harlem Renaissance and the New Negro Movement) may thus be seen as a response to pressures from both within and without the black community.

In fiction the peculiar mix of primitivism and cultural nationalism may be best seen in three novels of the West Indian born Claude McKay: HOME TO HARLEM (1928), BANJO (1929), and BANANA BOTTOM (1933), as well as in his collection of short stories, GINGERTOWN (1932). In these he wrote sympathetically of soldiers, longshoremen, pimps, prostitutes, dining car cooks, musicians, and the like. Some of these stories were set in France, some in the West Indies, and some in Harlem, but their heroes were always the same--the black underclass who had hitherto been despised or caricatured by an earlier generation of middle-class Negro writers. To a greater or lesser extent, similar portrayals and a consequent melange of ideologies and protest may be found in the short fiction and novels of Wallace Thurman, Rudolph Fisher, Langston Hughes, Arna Bontemps, and Countee Cullen. Meanwhile, what the writers were doing for the poor urban dweller, Jean Toomer was doing for the black Southern peasant and earthy black female in his curious novel, CANE. (1923). And while even respected figures like W.E.B. DuBois inveighed against what they regarded as the sensationalistic idealizing of blacks, DuBois himself would write a novel, DARK PRINCESS (1928), describing a future world-wide colored uprising.

There were also, of course, any number of authors who wrote about middle-class life or presented their accounts from a middle-class point of view: that is to say they were neither nationalists nor were they enamored of primitives. Their primary concerns were surviving emotionally in a racist world. One of the better of these writers was Nella Larsen, whose QUICKSAND (1928) describes the decline of a sensitive young woman of mixed parentage in a Southern backwoods community.

While one author of this period, Arna Bontemps, has argued that the Negro Renaissance never really ended, most scholars are agreed that the Depression years and World War II (1933-45) produced a different kind of Negro writing. Primarily it was a literature of social protest (Negro problems were an important by-product of the class struggle and not purely racial in origin), and its principal figure was Richard Wright. Elements of cultural and political nationalism may of course be discovered in Wright's work, but he regarded himself as a Marxist and his writings as examples of the Negro experience examined from a Marxist point of view. That Wright's work rose far above propaganda

may be attributed to his skill in narration and his adeptness at portraying iso-
lated rebellious Negro heroes (like himself) who felt at home neither with
blacks who had "adjusted" nor the white civilization that persecuted them.
Wright's most famous novel is the celebrated NATIVE SON (1940), but attention
should be drawn as well to his earlier collection of short stories and novellas,
UNCLE TOM'S CHILDREN (1938).

Here some kind of tenuous connection may be drawn between protest fiction and
the writings of the Negro Renaissance. Though Wright's stories are no doubt
socially oriented, their emphasis on the elevated nature of the Southern Negro
peasant is in some respects not unlike Toomer's idealizations. Closer still are
the novels and short fiction of Zora Neale Hurston (JONAH'S GOURD VINE
[1934] and THEIR EYES WERE WATCHING GOD [1937]) and George Wylie
Henderson (OLLIE MISS [1935]). These dealt with Southern rural life sans class
conflict. Perhaps the central transitional work is William Attaway's excellent
BLOOD ON THE FORGE (1941) that told of Kentucky farmers who went north
to Pittsburgh to work in the steel mills. Social protest, however, was carried
on in the fiction of Ann Petry (THE STREET [1946]), Chester Himes (IF HE
HOLLERS LET HIM GO [1946]), and Willard Motley (KNOCK ON ANY DOOR
[1947]), whose protagonist was white, as well as in the writings of a few lesser
figures. Although Wright and many of the above authors produced works well
into the 1950s and beyond, they made their major impact in the two preceding
decades.

The postwar years brought a new introspective quality to Afro-American literature. Social and racial issues were not forgotten, but authors appeared princi-
pally interested in exploring their psyches and in discovering or rediscovering
their black identities within the larger American context. The primary figures
of the 1950s in this regard are James Baldwin (GO TELL IT ON THE MOUN-
TAIN [1953]), and Ralph Ellison (INVISIBLE MAN [1952]). Although their works
are rich in social detail, their major concern is with their protagonists' coming
to terms with themselves in a world that denies them dignity or depth. In the
following decade both authors were frequently attacked by other blacks for not
being sufficiently militant or nationalistic, but in certain respects they continue
to represent the dominant trend in present day Afro-American fiction--a central concern for the integrity of the black psyche. A look at the titles of any
of the major fiction writers of the sixties and seventies should confirm this.
Some, of course, like William Demby (THE CATACOMBS [1965]), William
Melvin Kelley (DUNFORDS TRAVELS EVERYWHERES [1970]), Ishmael Reed
(MUMBO JUMBO [1972]) and John A. Williams (CAPTAIN BLACKMAN [1972])
may be more experimental. Some, however, like Ernest Gaines (BLOODLINE
[1968]), Toni Morrison (THE BLUEST EYE, [1970]), and Paule Marshall (BROWN
GIRL, BROWNSTONES, [1959]), are more traditional, returning to childhood or
youth to reexamine their identity. All have eschewed sacrificing their art on the
altar of this or that ideology; this is not to say that some are not ideological,
but none has surrendered his or her commitments to freedom and dignity. Indeed
by remaining true to themselves and their experiences, they have confirmed and
articulated the highest hopes of their literary ancestors, the writers of the slave
narratives.

## NOTES

1. Robert Bone, DOWN HOME (New York: G.P. Putnam's Sons, 1975), p. 3.

2. See, for example, James Weldon Johnson's AUTOBIOGRAPHY OF AN EX-COLORED MAN (1912) and Oscar Micheaux's THE CONQUEST (1913), both of which have confused critics as regards genre.

# ABBREVIATIONS OF PERIODICAL AND SERIAL TITLES

AL       AMERICAN LITERATURE

ALR      AMERICAN LITERARY REALISM, 1870-1910

ALS      AMERICAN LITERARY SCHOLARSHIP

AmerS    AMERICAN STUDIES (Formerly MIDCONTINENT AMERICAN STUDIES JOURNAL)

AR       ANTIOCH REVIEW

ASch     AMERICAN SCHOLAR

BB       BULLETIN OF BIBLIOGRAPHY

BlackW   BLACK WORLD (Formerly NEGRO DIGEST)

CLAJ     COLLEGE LANGUAGE ASSOCIATION JOURNAL (Morgan State Coll., Baltimore, Md.)

ConL     CONTEMPORARY LITERATURE (Supersedes WSCL)

Crit     CRITIQUE: STUDIES IN MODERN FICTION

IowaR    IOWA REVIEW

MarkR    MARKHAM REVIEW

MASJ     MIDCONTINENT AMERICAN STUDIES JOURNAL

MFS      MODERN FICTION STUDIES

MinnR    MINNESOTA REVIEW

MQR      MICHIGAN QUARTERLY REVIEW

MR       MASSACHUSETTS REVIEW

NALF     NEGRO AMERICAN LITERATURE FORUM

NewL     NEW LETTERS (Formerly UNIVERSITY REVIEW)

NYHTBW   NEW YORK HERALD TRIBUNE BOOK WEEK

NYRB     NEW YORK REVIEW OF BOOKS

NYTBR    NEW YORK TIMES BOOK REVIEW

# Abbreviations

| | |
|---|---|
| PR | PARTISAN REVIEW |
| RALS | RESOURCES FOR AMERICAN LITERARY STUDIES |
| SAF | STUDIES IN AMERICAN FICTION |
| SatR | SATURDAY REVIEW (Formerly SATURDAY REVIEW OF LITERATURE) |
| SBL | STUDIES IN BLACK LITERATURE |
| SCR | SOUTH CAROLINA REVIEW |
| SLitI | STUDIES IN THE LITERARY IMAGINATION (Ga. State Coll.) |
| SLJ | SOUTHERN LITERARY JOURNAL |
| SNNTS | STUDIES IN THE NOVEL (North Texas State) |
| SoR | SOUTHERN REVIEW (Louisiana State U.) |
| SSF | STUDIES IN SHORT FICTION |
| TCL | TWENTIETH-CENTURY LITERATURE |
| TriQ | TRI-QUARTERLY (Evanston, Ill.) |
| UKCR | UNIVERSITY OF KANSAS CITY REVIEW |
| VQR | VIRGINIA QUARTERLY REVIEW |
| WSCL | WISCONSIN STUDIES IN CONTEMPORARY LITERATURE |
| YULG | YALE UNIVERSITY LIBRARY GAZETTE |

# Chapter 1

# CHECKLIST OF NOVELS

The novels in this chapter are arranged alphabetically by author's name. Each author's work is listed chronologically. Juvenile literature is omitted. Included are many titles published privately or at the expense of the author. The reader is cautioned that some recent books dealing with sensational subject matter, such as pimping, drugs, and violent crimes, purport to be written by black authors but may in fact be frauds. We have tried to record only those we believe are authentic; however, in dealing with some of the less reputable publishing houses, there can be considerable margin of error.

Anonymously published works are entered under title. Titles printed abroad are cited only when American editions do not exist. As a rule we do not list reprints for novels and short story collections (except when title changes are noted as in entries 51 and 65); but the reader should be aware that in addition to the trade publishers, some houses have specialized in reproducing out-of-print works by Afro-Americans. Below are some houses whose catalogs the reader might consult:

AMS Press
56 East 13th Street
New York, N.Y.   10003

Chatham Bookseller
38 Maple Street
Chatham, N.J.   07928

Arno Press
3 Park Avenue
New York, N.Y.   10016

Xerox University Microfilms
300 North Zeeb Road
Ann Arbor, Mich.   48106

## NOVELS

1       Adams, Alger Leroy [pseud. Philip B. Kaye]. TAFFY. New York: Crown Publishers, 1950.

2       Adams, Clayton. See Holmes, Charles Henry.

3       Anderson, Alston. ALL GOD'S CHILDREN. Indianapolis, Ind.: Bobbs-Merrill, 1965.

# Checklist of Novels

4   Anderson, Henry L. NO USE CRYIN'. Los Angeles: Western Publishers, 1961.

5   Anderson, William H. See Stowers, Walter H.--joint author.

6   Arnold, Ethel Nishua. SHE KNEW NO EVIL. New York: Vantage Press, 1953.

7   Arthur, John. See Joseph, Arthur

8   Ashby, William Mobile. REDDER BLOOD. New York: Cosmopolitan Press, 1915.

9   Ashley, Martin. CHECKMATE AND DEATHMATE. New York: Vantage Press, 1973.

10   Atkins, Russell. MALEFICIUM. Cleveland, Ohio: Free Lance, 1971.

11   Attaway, William. LET ME BREATHE THUNDER. New York: Doubleday, Doran, 1939.

12   _____. BLOOD ON THE FORGE. Garden City, N.Y.: Doubleday, Doran, 1941.

13   Austin, Edmund O. THE BLACK CHALLENGE. New York: Vantage Press, 1958.

14   Baldwin, James. GO TELL IT ON THE MOUNTAIN. New York: Alfred A. Knopf, 1953.

15   _____. GIOVANNI'S ROOM. New York: Dial Press, 1956.

16   _____. ANOTHER COUNTRY. New York: Dial Press, 1962.

17   _____. TELL ME HOW LONG THE TRAIN'S BEEN GONE. New York: Dial Press, 1968.

18   _____. IF BEALE STREET COULD TALK. New York: Dial Press, 1974.

19   Barnes, Ben E. See Gay, Kathlyn--joint author.

20   Barrett, Nathan. BARS OF ADAMANT: A TROPICAL NOVEL. New York: Fleet, 1966.

21   Battle, Sol. MELANGE IN BLACK. New York: Panther House, 1970.

22   Battles, Jesse Moore. SOMEBODY PLEASE HELP ME. New York: Pageant Press, 1965.

23   Beason, Mattie. WEST TO THE OHIO RIVER. Los Angeles: Crescent Publications, 1976.

24   Beck, Robert [pseud. Iceberg Slim]. TRICK BABY. Los Angeles: Holloway House, 1967.

25   _____. [pseud. Iceberg Slim]. MAMA BLACK WIDOW. Los Angeles: Holloway House, 1969.

26   Beckham, Barry. MY MAIN MOTHER. New York: Walker & Co., 1969.

27   _____. RUNNER MACK. New York: William Morrow, 1972.

28   Bellinger, Claudia. WOLF KITTY. New York: Vantage Press, 1958.

29   Benjamin, R.C.O. THE DEFENDER OF OBADIAH CUFF. Cleveland, Ohio: N.p., 1887.

30   Bennett, Hal. A WILDERNESS OF VINES. Garden City, N.Y.: Doubleday, 1966.

31   _____. THE BLACK WINE. Garden City, N.Y.: Doubleday, 1968.

32   _____. LORD OF DARK PLACES. New York: W.W. Norton, 1970.

33   _____. WAIT UNTIL THE EVENING. Garden City, N.Y.: Doubleday, 1974.

34   _____. SEVENTH HEAVEN. Garden City, N.Y.: Doubleday, 1976.

35   Bernard, Ruth Thompson. WHAT'S WRONG WITH LOTTERY? Boston: Meador Publishing Co., 1943.

36   Blackson, Lorenzo D. THE RISE AND PROGRESS OF THE KINGDOMS OF LIGHT AND DARKNESS. Philadelphia: J. Nicholas, 1867.

37   Blackwood, Granby. UN SANG MAL MELE. Paris: Editions Denoel, 1966.

3

38    Blair, John Paul. DEMOCRACY REBORN. New York: F. Hubner and Co., 1946.

39    Bland, Alden. BEHOLD A CRY. New York: Charles Scribner's Sons, 1947.

40    Boles, Robert E. THE PEOPLE ONE KNOWS. Boston: Houghton Mifflin, 1964.

41    _____. CURLING. Boston: Houghton Mifflin, 1968.

42    Bond, Odessa. THE DOUBLE TRAGEDY. New York: Vantage Press, 1970.

43    Bontemps, Arna. GOD SENDS SUNDAY. New York: Harcourt, Brace, 1931.

44    _____. BLACK THUNDER. New York: Macmillan, 1936.

45    _____. DRUMS AT DUSK. New York: Macmillan, 1939.

46    Bosworth, William. THE LONG SEARCH. Great Barrington, Mass.: Advance Publishing Co., 1957.

47    Bottoms, Timothy L. MR. SCHUTZER. New York: Carlton Press, 1975.

48    Boullon, J.M. SURRENDER THE DREAM. Philadelphia: Dorrance, 1976.

49    Bradley, David. SOUTH STREET. New York: Grossman, 1975.

50    Branch, Edward. THE HIGH PLACES. New York: Exposition Press, 1957.

51    Bridgeford, Med. GOD'S LAW AND MAN'S. 1927; rpt. as ANOTHER CHANCE. New York: Exposition Press, 1951.

52    Briscoe, Lawrance. FISHER'S ALLEY. New York: Vantage Press, 1973.

53    Broadus, Robert Deal. SPOKES FOR THE WHEEL. Muncie, Ind.: Kingsman Press, 1961.

54    Brocket, Joshua Arthur. ZIPPORAH, THE MAID OF MIDIAN. Zion, Ill.: Zion Printing and Publishing House, [1926].

55    Brooks, Gwendolyn. MAUD MARTHA. New York: Harper & Brothers, 1953.

56    Brown, Cecil. THE LIFE AND LOVES OF MR. JIVEASS NIGGER. New York: Farrar, Straus & Giroux, 1969.

57    Brown, Charlotte Hawkins. "MAMMY," AN APPEAL TO THE HEART OF THE SOUTH. Boston: Pilgrim Press, 1919.

58    Brown, Frank London. TRUMBULL PARK. Chicago: Henry Regnery, 1959.

59    _____. THE MYTH MAKER. Chicago: Path Press, 1969.

60    Brown, Handy Nereus. THE NECROMANCER. Opelika, Ala.: N.p., 1904.

61    Brown, Josephine Stephens. THE WAY OF THE SHADOWS. New York: Exposition Press, 1973.

62    Brown, Lloyd L. IRON CITY. New York: Masses & Mainstream, 1951.

63    Brown, Mattye Jeanette. THE REIGN OF TERROR. New York: Vantage Press, 1962.

64    Brown, Theodore. THE BAND WILL NOT PLAY DIXIE. New York: Exposition Press, 1955.

65    Brown, William Wells. CLOTEL; OR, THE PRESIDENT'S DAUGHTER: A NARRATIVE OF SLAVE LIFE IN THE UNITED STATES. London: Partridge & Oakey, 1853. Rev. and retitled MIRALDA; OR, THE BEAUTIFUL QUADROON, published in THE WEEKLY ANGLO-AFRICAN, November 30, 1860 - March 16, 1861. Also as CLOTELLE: A TALE OF THE SOUTHERN STATES. Boston: James Redpath, 1864, and CLOTELLE; OR, THE COLORED HEROINE, A TALE OF THE SOUTHERN STATES. Boston: Lee & Shepard, 1867.

66    Bruce, John Edward. THE AWAKENING OF HEZEKIAH JONES. Hopkinsville, Ky.: Phil H. Brown Publishing Co., 1916.

# Checklist of Novels

67  Bullins, Ed. THE RELUCTANT RAPIST. New York: Harper & Row, 1973.

68  Bush, Olivia Ward. DRIFTWOOD. Providence, R.I.: Atlantic Printing Co., 1914.

   Poetry and prose.

69  Buster, Greene. BRIGHTER SUN. New York: Pageant Press, 1954.

70  Butler, Octavia E. PATTERNMASTER. Garden City, N.Y.: Doubleday, 1976.

71  Byer, Reggie. NOBODY GETS RICH. New York: Vantage Press, 1975.

72  Cain, George. BLUESCHILD BABY. New York: McGraw-Hill, 1970.

73  Cain, Johnnie Mae. WHITE BASTARDS. New York: Vantage Press, 1973.

74  Caldwell, Lewis A.H. THE POLICY KING. Chicago: New Vistas Publishing House, 1945.

75  Cannon, Steve. GROOVE, BANG AND JIVE AROUND. New York: Ophelia Press, 1969.

76  Carrere, Mentis. MAN IN THE CANE. New York: Vantage Press, 1956.

77  _____. IT'S ALL SOUTH. Los Angeles: John Henry and Mary Louisa Dunn Bryant Foundation, 1966.

   The novel appeared in the form of four short pamphlets, not one volume.

78  Carson, Lular L. THE PRICELESS GIFT. New York: Vantage Press, 1970.

79  Carvalho, Grimaldo. THE NEGRO MESSIAH. New York: Vantage Press, 1969.

80  Chantrelle, Seginald. NOT WITHOUT DUST. New York: Exposition Press, 1954.

81  Cheatwood, Kiarri. LIGHTNING IN THE SWAMP. Detroit: Agascha Productions, 1976.

82    Chesnut, Robert. See Cooper, Clarence L., Jr.

83    Chesnutt, Charles Waddell. THE HOUSE BEHIND THE CEDARS. Boston and New York: Houghton Mifflin, 1900.

      See also Micheaux, entry 430.

84    _____. THE MARROW OF TRADITION. Boston and New York: Houghton Mifflin, 1901.

85    _____. THE COLONEL'S DREAM. New York: Doubleday, Page & Company, 1905.

86    Clark, Al C. See Goines, Donald.

87    Clinton, Dorothy Randle. THE MADDENING SCAR. Boston: Christopher Publishing House, 1962.

88    Coleman, Albert Evander. THE ROMANTIC ADVENTURES OF ROSY, THE OCTOROON. Boston: Meador Publishing Co., 1929.

89    Coleman, James Nelson. THE NULL-FREQUENCY IMPULSER. New York: Berkley, 1959.

90    _____. SEEKER FROM THE STARS. New York: Berkley, 1967.

91    Coleman, Merton H. THAT GODLESS WOMAN. New York: Vantage Press, 1969.

92    Colter, Cyrus. THE RIVERS OF EROS. Chicago: Swallow Press, 1972.

93    _____. THE HIPPODROME. Chicago: Swallow Press, 1973.

94    CONFESSIONS OF A NEGRO PREACHER. Chicago: Canterbury Press, 1928.

95    Cook, Douglas. CHOKER'S SON. New York: Comet Press, 1959.

96    Cooke, W.C. THE RUNGLESS LADDER. New York: Exposition Press, 1960.

97    Coolidge, Fay Liddle. BLACK IS WHITE. New York: Vantage Press, 1958.

98      Cooper, Clarence L., Jr. THE SYNDICATE.
        Copy not located. Ca. 1956–60. The list of Cooper's works
        in THE FARM cites SYNDICATE as published under the name
        of Robert Chesnut.

99      _____. THE SCENE. New York: Crown Publishers, 1960.

100     _____. WEED. Evanston, Ill.: Regency, 1961.

101     _____. THE DARK MESSENGER. Evanston, Ill.: Regency, 1962.

102     _____. BLACK! TWO SHORT NOVELS. Evanston, Ill.: Regency,
        1963.

103     _____. THE FARM. New York: Crown Publishers, 1967.

104     Cooper, John L. OPUS ONE. New York: Maelstrom, 1966.

105     Cooper, William. THANK GOD FOR A SONG. New York: Exposi-
        tion Press, 1962.

106     Corbo, D.R., Jr. HARD GROUND. New York: Vantage Press, 1954.

107     Cotton, Donald J. SORE FOOTS. Washington, D.C.: Libratterian
        Books, 1972.

108     Cotton, Ella Earls. QUEEN OF PERSIA. New York: Exposition Press,
        1960.

109     Cox, Joseph Mason Andrew. THE SEARCH. New York: Daniel S.
        Mead, 1960.

110     Crump, George Peter, Jr. FROM BONDAGE THEY CAME. New York:
        Vantage Press, 1954.

111     Crump, Paul. BURN, KILLER, BURN! Chicago: Johnson Publishing
        Co., 1962.

112     Cullen, Countee. ONE WAY TO HEAVEN. New York: Harper &
        Brothers, 1932.

113     Cunningham, George, Jr. LILY-SKIN LOVER. New York: Exposition
        Press, 1960.

114    Daly, Victor. NOT ONLY WAR, A STORY OF TWO GREAT CON-
       FLICTS. Boston: Christopher Publishing House, 1932.

115    Davis, Charles. TWO WEEKS TO FIND A KILLER. New York: Carl-
       ton Press, 1966.

116    Davis, Charles W. THE NUT AND BOLT. New York: Vantage Press,
       1972.

117    Davis, George. COMING HOME. New York: Random House, 1971.

118    Davis, Joseph A. BLACK BONDAGE: A NOVEL OF A DOOMED
       NEGRO IN TODAY'S SOUTH. New York: Exposition Press, 1959.

119    Davis, Nolan. SIX BLACK HORSES. New York: G.P. Putnam's
       Sons, 1971.

120    Dee, John. STAGGER LEE. New York: Manor Books, 1973.

121    Delany, Martin R. BLAKE, OR THE HUTS OF AMERICA. Boston:
       Beacon Press, 1970.

       This book was partly serialized in THE ANGLO-AFRICAN,
       New York, January 1859 (the magazine's first issue) with six
       additional installments through July 1859. These twenty-six
       published chapters and forty-eight additional chapters were
       published in THE WEEKLY ANGLO-AFRICAN, November 26,
       1861 through late May 1862. The novel was, however, still
       incomplete, lacking approximately six chapters. The 1970 Bea-
       con Press edition contains the seventy-four previously published
       chapters with an appeal to readers for any information regard-
       ing the whereabouts of the missing six chapters.

122    Delany, Samuel R. THE JEWELS OF APTOR. New York: Ace, 1962.

123    _____. THE TOWERS OF TORON. New York: Ace, 1964.

124    _____. THE BALLAD OF BETA-2. New York: Ace, 1965.

125    _____. CAPTIVES OF THE FLAME. New York: Ace, 1965.

126    _____. CITY OF A THOUSAND SUNS. New York: Ace, 1965.

127    _____. BABEL-17. New York: Ace, 1966.

128 _____. EMPIRE STAR. New York: Ace, 1966.

129 _____. THE EINSTEIN INTERSECTION. New York: Ace, 1967.

130 _____. NOVA. Garden City, N.Y.: Doubleday, 1968.

131 _____. THE FALL OF THE TOWERS. New York: Ace, 1970.
Revision of earlier trilogy-- THE TOWERS OF TORON, CAP-
TIVES OF THE FLAME, and CITY OF A THOUSAND SUNS.

132 _____. THE TIDES OF LUST. New York: Lancer, 1973.

133 _____. DHALGREN. New York: Bantam Books, 1975.

134 _____. TRITON. New York: Bantam Books, 1976.

135 Demby, William. BEETLECREEK. New York: Rinehart, 1950.

136 _____. LA SETTIMANA DELLA FEDE. Rome: Atlante, 1952.

137 _____. THE CATACOMBS. New York: Pantheon Books, 1965.

138 Detter, Thomas. NELLIE BROWN, OR THE JEALOUS WIFE. San
Francisco: Cuddy and Hughes, 1871.

139 Dickens, Al. UNCLE YAH YAH. Detroit: Harlo Press, 1976.

140 Dickens, Dorothy Lee. BLACK ON THE RAINBOW. New York:
Pageant Press, 1952.

141 Diggs, Arthur. BLACK WOMAN. New York: Exposition Press, 1954.

142 Dodson, Owen. BOY AT THE WINDOW. New York: Farrar, Straus
& Young, 1951; rpt. as WHEN TREES ARE GREEN. New York:
Popular Library, 1967.

143 Dorsey, John T. THE LION OF JUDAH. Chicago: Fouche Co., 1924.

144 Downing, Henry F. THE AMERICAN CAVALRYMAN. New York:
Neale, 1917.

145    Dreer, Herman. THE IMMEDIATE JEWEL OF HIS SOUL. St. Louis, Mo.: St. Louis Argus Publishing Co., 1919.

146    _____. THE TIE THAT BINDS. Boston: Meador Publishing Co., 1958.

147    Drummond, Mary. COME GO WITH ME. Philadelphia: Dorrance, 1973.

148    Du Bois, David Graham. . . AND BID HIM SING. Palo Alto, Calif.: Ramparts Press, 1976.

149    DuBois, Shirley Graham (Shirley Graham). ZULU HEART. New York: Third Press, 1974.

150    DuBois, W.E.B. THE QUEST OF THE SILVER FLEECE. Chicago: A.C. McClurg & Co., 1911.

151    _____. DARK PRINCESS. New York: Harcourt, Brace, 1928.

152    _____. THE ORDEAL OF MANSART. New York: Mainstream Publishers, 1957.

       Book One of THE BLACK FLAME, a trilogy.

153    _____. MANSART BUILDS A SCHOOL. New York: Mainstream Publishers, 1959.

       Book Two of THE BLACK FLAME, a trilogy.

154    _____. WORLDS OF COLOR. New York: Mainstream Publishers, 1961.

       Book Three of THE BLACK FLAME, a trilogy.

155    Dumas, Henry. JONOAH AND THE GREEN STONE. New York: Random House, 1976.

156    Dunbar, Paul Laurence. THE UNCALLED. New York: Dodd, Mead, 1898.

157    _____. THE LOVE OF LANDRY. New York: Dodd, Mead, 1900.

158    _____. THE FANATICS. New York: Dodd, Mead, 1901.

159 _____. THE SPORT OF THE GODS. New York: Dodd, Mead, 1902.

160 Durant, E. Elliott, and Cuthbert M. Roach. THE PRINCESS OF NA-RAGPUR, OR A DAUGHTER OF ALLAH. New York: Grafton Press, 1928.

161 Durham, John Stephens. DIANE, PRINCESS OF HAITI. Philadelphia: LIPPINCOTT'S MONTHLY MAGAZINE, April 1902.

162 Earle, Victoria (Victoria Earle Matthews). AUNT LINDY, A STORY FOUNDED ON REAL LIFE. New York: Press of J.J. Little & Co., 1893.

163 Easley, Nivi-Kofi A. THE MILITANTS. New York: Carlton Press, 1974.

164 Easterling, Renee. A STRANGE WAY HOME. New York: Pageant Press, 1952.

165 Edwards, Junius. IF WE MUST DIE. Garden City, N.Y.: Doubleday, 1963.

166 Edwards, S.W. See Sublette, Walter E.

167 Ellis, George Washington. THE LEOPARD'S CLAW. New York: International Author's Association, 1917.

168 Ellis, Teresa. NO WAY BACK: A NOVELLA. New York: Exposition Press, 1973.

169 Ellison, Ralph. INVISIBLE MAN. New York: Random House, 1952.

170 English, Rubynn M. CITIZEN, U.S.A. New York: Pageant Press, 1957.

171 Fair, Ronald. MANY THOUSAND GONE. New York: Harcourt, Brace & World, 1965.

172 _____. HOG BUTCHER. New York: Harcourt, Brace & World, 1966.

173 _____. WORLD OF NOTHING: TWO NOVELLAS. New York: Harper & Row, 1970.

174 _____. WE CAN'T BREATHE. New York: Harper & Row, 1972.

175    Fairley, Ruth A. ROCKS AND ROSES. New York: Vantage Press, 1970.

176    Farmer, Clarence. SOUL ON FIRE. New York: Belmont Books, 1969.

177    Farrell, John T. THE NAKED TRUTH. New York: Vantage Press, 1961.

178    Faulkner, Blanche. THE LIVELY HOUSE. Los Angeles: Crescent Publications, 1975.

179    Fauset, Jessie R. THERE IS CONFUSION. New York: Boni and Liveright, 1924.

180    _____. PLUM BUN. New York: Frederick A. Stokes Co., 1929.

181    _____. THE CHINABERRY TREE. New York: Frederick A. Stokes Co., 1931.

182    _____. COMEDY, AMERICAN STYLE. New York: Frederick A. Stokes Co., 1933.

183    Felton, James A. FRUITS OF ENDURING FAITH. New York: Exposition Press, 1965.

184    Ferguson, Ira Lunan. OCEE McRAE, TEXAS. New York: Exposition Press, 1962.

185    _____. THE BIOGRAPHY OF G. WASH CARTER, WHITE. San Francisco: Lunan-Ferguson Library, 1969.

186    Finch, Amanda. BACK TRAIL: A NOVELLA OF LOVE IN THE SOUTH. New York: William-Frederick Press, 1951.

187    Fiore, Carmen Anthony. THE BARRIER. New York: Pageant Press, 1965.

188    Fisher, Rudolph. THE WALLS OF JERICHO. New York: Alfred A. Knopf, 1928.

189    _____. THE CONJURE MAN DIES. New York: Covici-Friede, 1932.

190    Fisher, William. THE WAITERS. Cleveland, Ohio: World, 1953.

191  Fleming, Sarah Lee Brown. HOPE'S HIGHWAY. New York: Neale, 1917.

192  Flemister, John T. FURLOUGH FROM HELL, A FANTASY. New York: Exposition Press, 1964.

193  Forget-Me-Not. See Kelley, Emma Dunham.

194  Forrest, Leon. THERE IS A TREE MORE ANCIENT THAN EDEN. New York: Random House, 1973.

195  Forster, Christine. See Forte, Christine.

196  Forte, Christine [pseud. Christine Forster]. A VIEW FROM THE HILL. New York: Vantage Press, 1964.

197  _____. [pseud. Christine Forster]. YOUNG TIM O'HARA. New York: Vantage Press, 1966.

198  Fowler, Charles H. HISTORICAL ROMANCE OF THE AMERICAN NEGRO. Baltimore, Md.: Press of Thomas & Evans, 1902.

199  Fullilove, Maggie. WHO WAS RESPONSIBLE? Cincinnati, Ohio: Abingdon Press, 1919.

200  Gaines, Edwina. YOUR PEOPLE ARE MY PEOPLE. London: Great Western Publishing Co., 1962.

201  Gaines, Ernest J. CATHERINE CARMIER. New York: Atheneum Publishers, 1964.

202  _____. OF LOVE AND DUST. New York: Dial Press, 1967.

203  _____. THE AUTOBIOGRAPHY OF MISS JANE PITTMAN. New York: Dial Press, 1971.

204  Garrett, Beatrice. WELFARE ON SKID ROW. New York: Exposition Press, 1974.

205  Gary, Madeleine Sophie. VIGNETTES OF THE BEAM IN A NIGGER'S EYE. New York: Exposition Press, 1970.

206  Gay, Kathlyn, and Ben E. Barnes. THE RIVER FLOWS BACKWARDS. Port Washington, N.Y.: Ashley Books, 1975.

207 Gholson, Edward. FROM JERUSALEM TO JERICHO. Boston: Chapman & Grimes, 1943.

208 Gibson, Richard. A MIRROR FOR MAGISTRATES. London: Blond, 1958.

209 Gilbert, Herman Cromwell. THE UNCERTAIN SOUND. Chicago: Path, 1969.

210 Gilbert, Mercedes. AUNT SARAH'S WOODEN GOD. Boston: Christopher Publishing House, 1938.

211 Gilmore, F. Grant. "THE PROBLEM": A MILITARY NOVEL. Rochester, N.Y.: Press of Henry Conolly Co., 1915.

212 Gilmore, J. Lance. HELL HAS NO EXIT. Los Angeles: Holloway House, 1976.

213 Girard, James P. CHANGING ALL THOSE CHANGES. Berkeley, Calif.: Yardbird Wing Editions, 1976.

214 Gober, Dom. See Nazel, Joseph.

215 Goines, Donald. DOPEFIEND, THE STORY OF A BLACK JUNKIE. Los Angeles: Holloway House, 1971.

216 _____. WHORESON, THE STORY OF A GHETTO PIMP. Los Angeles: Holloway House, 1972.

217 _____. BLACK GANGSTER. Los Angeles: Holloway House, 1972.

218 _____. STREET PLAYERS. Los Angeles: Holloway House, 1973.

219 _____. WHITE MAN'S JUSTICE, BLACK MAN'S GRIEF. Los Angeles: Holloway House, 1973.

220 _____. BLACK GIRL LOST. Los Angeles: Holloway House, 1973.

221 _____. ELDORADO RED. Los Angeles: Holloway House, 1974.

222 _____. SWAMP MAN. Los Angeles: Holloway House, 1974.

223 _____. NEVER DIE ALONE. Los Angeles: Holloway House, 1974.

224 _____ [pseud. Al C. Clark]. CRIME PARTNERS. Los Angeles: Holloway House, 1974.

225 _____ [pseud. Al C. Clark]. DEATH LIST. Los Angeles: Holloway House, 1974.

226 _____. DADDY COOL. Los Angeles: Holloway House, 1974.

227 _____ [pseud. Al C. Clark]. CRY REVENGE! Los Angeles: Holloway House, 1974.

228 _____ [pseud. Al C. Clark]. KENYATTA'S ESCAPE. Los Angeles: Holloway House, 1975.

229 _____ [pseud. Al C. Clark]. KENYATTA'S LAST HIT. Los Angeles: Holloway House, 1975.

230 _____. INNER CITY HOODLUM. Los Angeles: Holloway House, 1975.

231 Graham, Katherine Campbell. UNDER THE COTTONWOOD. New York: Wendell Malliet Co., 1941.

232 Graham, Shirley. See DuBois, Shirley Graham.

233 Grant, John Wesley. OUT OF THE DARKNESS; OR, DIABOLISM AND DESTINY. Nashville, Tenn.: National Baptist Publishing Board, 1909.

234 Gray, Wade S. HER LAST PERFORMANCE. Omaha, Neb.: Rapid Printing and Publishing, 1944.

235 Greene, Joe [pseud. B.B. Johnson]. SUPERSPADE NO. 1: DEATH OF A BLUE-EYED SOUL BROTHER. New York: Paperback Library, 1970.

236 _____ [pseud. B.B. Johnson]. SUPERSPADE NO. 2: BLACK IS BEAUTIFUL. New York: Paperback Library, 1970.

237 _____ [pseud. B.B. Johnson]. SUPERSPADE NO. 3: THAT'S WHERE THE CAT'S AT, BABY. New York: Paperback Library, 1970.

238 _____ [pseud. B.B. Johnson]. SUPERSPADE NO. 4: MOTHER OF THE YEAR. New York: Paperback Library, 1970.

239 _____ [pseud. B.B. Johnson]. SUPERSPADE NO. 5: BAD DAY FOR A BLACK BROTHER. New York: Paperback Library, 1970.

240 _____ [pseud. B.B. Johnson]. SUPERSPADE NO. 6: BLUES FOR A BLACK SISTER. New York: Paperback Library, 1971.

241 Greenlee, Sam. THE SPOOK WHO SAT BY THE DOOR. New York: Richard W. Baron, 1969.

242 _____. BAGHDAD BLUES. New York: Bantam Books, 1976.

   The hardcover edition scheduled for publication by Emerson Hall, New York, 1973, never appeared.

243 Griggs, Sutton E. IMPERIUM IN IMPERIO. Cincinnati, Ohio: Editor Publishing Co., 1899.

244 _____. OVERSHADOWED. Nashville, Tenn.: Orion Publishing Co., 1901.

245 _____. UNFETTERED, A NOVEL. Nashville, Tenn.: Orion Publishing Co., 1902.

246 _____. THE HINDERED HAND; OR, THE REIGN OF THE REPRESSIONIST. Nashville, Tenn.: Orion Publishing Co., 1905.

247 _____. POINTING THE WAY. Nashville, Tenn.: Orion Publishing Co., 1908.

248 Gross, Werter L. THE GOLDEN RECOVERY. Reno, Nev.: Golden Recovery Corp., 1946.

249 Groves, John Wesley, IV. SHELLBREAK. New York: Paperback Library, 1970.

250 Gunn, Bill. ALL THE REST HAVE DIED. New York: Delacorte, 1964.

251 Guy, Rosa. BIRD AT MY WINDOW. Philadelphia: J.B. Lippincott, 1966.

252 _____. RUBY. New York: Random House, 1976.

253 Hagan, Willie. THE BLACK TARNISHED IMAGE. New York: Vantage Press, 1974.

254    Harper, Frances Ellen Watkins. IOLA LEROY; OR, SHADOWS UP-LIFTED. Philadelphia: Garrigues Brothers, 1892.

255    Harris, Charlie Avery. MACKING GANGSTER. Los Angeles: Holloway House, 1976.

256    _____. WHOREDAUGHTER. Los Angeles: Holloway House, 1976.

257    Harris, Elbert L. THE ATHENIAN. Daytona Beach, Fla.: College Publishing Co., 1956.

258    Harris, James L. ENDURANCE. New York: Vantage Press, 1973.

259    Harris, Leon R. RUN ZEBRA RUN! New York: Exposition Press, 1959.

260    Hart, Marcus A. THE LOVER WITH A KILLER'S INSTINCT. New York: Exposition Press, 1975.

261    Haskins, LeRoi Rosetti. THE WEAK ARM OF JUSTICE. New York: Vantage Press, 1971.

262    Hathorn, Christine. THE UNDOING OF MISS ABAGAIL WRIGLEY. New York: Vantage Press, 1973.

263    Hawkins, Odie. GHETTO SKETCHES. Los Angeles: Holloway House, 1972.

264    Heard, Nathan C. HOWARD STREET. New York: Dial Press, 1968.

265    _____. TO REACH A DREAM. New York: Dial Press, 1972.

266    _____. A COLD FIRE BURNING. New York: Simon and Schuster, 1974.

267    Heath, Eric. See Spence, Tomas H.--joint author.

268    Henderson, George Wylie. OLLIE MISS. New York: Frederick A. Stokes Co., 1935.

269    _____. JULE. New York: Creative Age Press, 1946.

270    Henry, William S. OUT OF WEDLOCK. Boston: R.G. Badger, 1931.

271   Hercules, Frank. WHERE THE HUMMINGBIRD FLIES. New York: Harcourt, Brace, 1961.

272   _____. I WANT A BLACK DOLL. New York: Simon and Schuster, 1967.

273   Hernton, Calvin. SCARECROW. Garden City, N.Y.: Doubleday, 1974.

274   Hill, John H. PRINCESS MALAH. Washington, D.C.: Associated Publishers, 1933.

275   Himes, Chester. IF HE HOLLERS LET HIM GO. Garden City, N.Y.: Doubleday, Doran, 1945.

276   _____. LONELY CRUSADE. New York: Alfred A. Knopf, 1947.

277   _____. CAST THE FIRST STONE. New York: Coward-McCann, 1952.

278   _____. THE THIRD GENERATION. Cleveland, Ohio: World, 1954.

279   _____. THE PRIMITIVE. New York: New American Library, 1955.

280   _____. FOR LOVE OF IMABELLE. Greenwich, Conn.: Fawcett, 1975; rpt. as A RAGE IN HARLEM. New York: Avon Books, 1965.

281   _____. THE CRAZY KILL. New York: Avon Books, 1959.

282   _____. THE REAL COOL KILLERS. New York: Avon Books, 1959.

283   _____. ALL SHOT UP. New York: Avon Books, 1960.

284   _____. THE BIG GOLD DREAM. New York: Avon Books, 1960.

285   _____. PINKTOES. Paris: Olympia Press, 1961 (first English language publication); rpt. New York: G.P. Putnam's Sons, Stein and Day, 1965 (first American published edition).

286   _____. UNE AFFAIRE DE VIOL. Paris: Editions les Yeux Ouverts, 1963.

287   _____. COTTON COMES TO HARLEM. New York: G.P. Putnam's Sons, 1965.

288 _____. THE HEAT'S ON. New York: G.P. Putnam's Sons, 1966.

289 _____. RUN MAN RUN. New York: G.P. Putnam's Sons, 1966.

290 _____. BLIND MAN WITH A PISTOL. New York: William Morrow, 1969; rpt. as HOT DAY, HOT NIGHT. New York: Dell, 1970.

291 Hodges, George W. SWAMP ANGEL. New York: New Voices, 1958.

292 Holmes, Charles Henry [pseud. Clayton Adams]. ETHIOPIA, THE LAND OF PROMISE. New York: Cosmopolitan Press, 1917.

293 Hooks, Nathaniel. TOWN ON TRIAL. New York: Exposition Press, 1959.

294 Hopkins, Pauline E. CONTENDING FORCES: A ROMANCE ILLUSTRA-TIVE OF NEGRO LIFE NORTH AND SOUTH. Boston: Colored Co-operative Publishing Co., 1900.

295 _____. WINONA: A TALE OF NEGRO LIFE IN THE SOUTH AND SOUTHWEST. (Serialized in COLORED AMERICAN MAGAZINE, May 1902-October 1902, vol. 5, nos. 1-6).

   This novel never appeared in book form.

296 _____. OF ONE BLOOD; OR, THE HIDDEN SELF. (Serialized in COLORED AMERICAN MAGAZINE, November 1902-November 1903, vol. 6, nos. 1-11.

   This novel never appeared in book form.

297 Horsman, Gallan. THE NOOSE AND THE SPEAR. New York: Vantage Press, 1965.

298 Hough, Florenz H. BLACK PARADISE. Philadelphia: Dorrance, 1953.

299 Howard, James H.W. BOND AND FREE; A TRUE TALE OF SLAVE TIMES. Harrisburg, Pa.: Edwin K. Meyers, 1886.

300 Huffman, Eugene Henry. "NOW I AM CIVILIZED." Los Angeles: Wetzel Publishing Co., 1930.

301 Hughes, Langston. NOT WITHOUT LAUGHTER. New York: Alfred A. Knopf, 1930.

302     \_\_\_\_\_. TAMBOURINES TO GLORY. New York: John Day, 1958.

303     Humphrey, Lillie Muse. AGGIE. New York: Vantage Press, 1955.

304     Hunter, H.L. THE MIRACLES OF THE RED ALTAR CLOTH. New York: Exposition Press, 1949.

305     Hunter, Helen. MAGNIFICENT WHITE MEN. New York: Vantage Press, 1964.

306     Hunter, Kristin. GOD BLESS THE CHILD. New York: Charles Scribner's Sons, 1964.

307     \_\_\_\_\_. THE LANDLORD. New York: Charles Scribner's Sons, 1966.

308     \_\_\_\_\_. THE SURVIVORS. New York: Charles Scribner's Sons, 1975.

309     Hurston, Zora Neale. JONAH'S GOURD VINE. Philadelphia: J.B. Lippincott, 1934.

310     \_\_\_\_\_. THEIR EYES WERE WATCHING GOD. Philadelphia: J.B. Lippincott, 1937.

311     \_\_\_\_\_. MOSES, MAN OF THE MOUNTAIN. Philadelphia: J.B. Lippincott, 1939.

312     \_\_\_\_\_. SERAPH ON THE SUWANEE. New York: Charles Scribner's Sons, 1948.

313     Iceberg Slim. See Beck, Robert.

314     Imbert, Dennis F. THE COLORED GENTLEMEN. New Orleans: Williams Printing Service, 1931.

315     Jackson, Blyden. OPERATION BURNING CANDLE. New York: Third Press, 1973.

316     \_\_\_\_\_. TOTEM. New York: Third Press, 1975.

317     Jackson, Emma Lou. THE VEIL OF NANCY. New York: Carlton Press, 1970.

318     Jackson, J. Denis [pseud. Julian Moreau]. THE BLACK COMMANDOS. Atlanta, Ga.: Cultural Institute Press, 1967.

319    Jackson, W. Warner. THE BIRTH OF THE MARTYR'S GHOST. New York: Comet Press, 1957.

320    James, Beauregard. THE ROAD TO BIRMINGHAM. New York: Bridge-head Books, 1964.

321    Janssen, Milton W. DIVIDED. New York: Pageant Press, 1963.

322    Jarrett, A.Q. BENEATH THE SKY. New York: Weinberg Book Supply, 1949.

323    Jarry, Hawke. BLACK SCHOOLMASTER. New York: Exposition Press, 1970.

324    Jefferson, Roland S. THE SCHOOL ON 103RD STREET. New York: Vantage Press, 1976.

325    Jenkins, Deaderick Franklin. IT WAS NOT MY WORLD. Los Angeles: Privately printed, 1942.

326    _____. LETTERS TO MY SON. Los Angeles: Deaderick F[ranklin]. Jenkins Publishing Co., 1947.

327    Jezebelle. See Smith, Lois A.

328    Johnson, Amelia E. THE HAZELEY FAMILY. Philadelphia: American Baptist Publication Society, 1894.

329    _____. MARTINA MERIDEN, OR WHAT IS MY MOTIVE? Philadelphia: American Baptist Publication Society, 1901.

330    Johnson, B.B. See Greene, Joe.

331    Johnson, Charles. FAITH AND THE GOOD THING. New York: Viking Press, 1974.

332    Johnson, Edward Augustus. LIGHT AHEAD FOR THE NEGRO. New York: Grafton Press, 1904.

333    Johnson, Eugene D. OF HUMAN KINDNESS. New York: Vantage Press, 1975.

334    Johnson, Evelyn Allen. MY NEIGHBOR'S ISLAND. New York: Exposition Press, 1965.

335 Johnson, Henry Theodore. KEY TO THE PROBLEM. Philadelphia: A.M.E. Book Concern, 1904.

336 Johnson, Hubert E., and Loretta Johnson. POPPY. New York: Carlton Press, 1969.

337 Johnson, James Weldon. THE AUTOBIOGRAPHY OF AN EX-COLORED MAN. Boston: Sherman, French and Co., 1912.

First edition published anonymously.

338 Johnson, Joe. COURTIN', SPORTIN', AND NON-SUPPORTIN'. New York: Vantage Press, 1965.

339 Johnson, Loretta. See Johnson, Hubert E.--joint author.

340 Johnson, William M. THE HOUSE ON CORBETT STREET. New York: William-Frederick Press, 1967.

341 Jones, Gayl. CORREGIDORA. New York: Random House, 1975.

342 _____. EVA'S MAN. New York: Random House, 1976.

343 Jones, J. McHenry. HEARTS OF GOLD. Wheeling, W. Va.: Daily Intelligencer Steam Job Press, 1896.

344 Jones, Joshua Henry, Jr. BY SANCTION OF LAW. Boston: B.J. Brimner, 1924.

345 Jones, LeRoi. THE SYSTEM OF DANTE'S HELL. New York: Grove Press, 1965.

346 Jones, Ralph H. THE PEPPERPOT MAN. New York: Vantage Press, 1965.

347 Jones, William H. THE TRIANGLE'S END. New York: Exposition Press, 1954.

348 Jones, Yorke. THE CLIMBERS. Chicago: Glad Tidings Publishing Co., 1912.

349 Jordan, Elsie. STRANGE SINNER. New York: Pageant Press, 1954.

350 Jordan, June. HIS OWN WHERE. New York: Thomas Y. Crowell, 1971.

351    Jordan, Moses. THE MEAT MAN. Chicago: Judy Publishing Co., 1923.

352    Joseph, Arthur [pseud. John Arthur]. DARK METROPOLIS. Boston: Meador Publishing Co., 1936.

353    _____ [pseud. John Arthur]. VOLCANO IN OUR MIDST. New York: Pageant Press, 1952.

354    Kaye, Philip B. See Adams, Alger Leroy.

355    Kelley, Emma Dunham [pseud. Forget-Me-Not]. MEGDA. Boston: James H. Earle, 1892.

356    Kelley, William Melvin. A DIFFERENT DRUMMER. Garden City, N.Y.: Doubleday, 1962.

357    _____. A DROP OF PATIENCE. Garden City, N.Y.: Doubleday, 1965.

358    _____. DEM. Garden City, N.Y.: Doubleday, 1967.

359    _____. DUNFORDS TRAVELS EVERYWHERES. Garden City, N.Y.: Doubleday, 1970.

360    Kemp, Arnold. EAT OF ME, I AM THE SAVIOR. New York: William Morrow, 1972.

361    Kennedy, Mark. THE PECKING ORDER. New York: Appleton-Century-Crofts, 1953.

362    Killens, John Oliver. YOUNGBLOOD. New York: Dial Press, 1954.

363    _____. AND THEN WE HEARD THE THUNDER. New York: Alfred A. Knopf, 1963.

364    _____. 'SIPPI. New York: Trident Press, 1967.

365    _____. SLAVES. New York: Pyramid Books, 1969.

366    _____. THE COTILLION, OR ONE GOOD BULL IS HALF THE HERD. New York: Trident Press, 1971.

367 Kimbrough, Jess. DEFENDER OF THE ANGELS. New York: Macmillan, 1969.

368 Kirk, Paul. NO NEED TO CRY. New York: Carlton Press, 1967.

369 Koiner, Richard B. JACK BE QUICK. New York: Lyle Stuart, 1966.

370 Kytle, Elizabeth. WILLIE MAE. New York: Alfred A. Knopf, 1958.

371 Lahon, Vyola Therese. THE BIG LIE. New York: Vantage Press, 1964.

372 Larsen, Nella. QUICKSAND. New York: Alfred A. Knopf, 1928.

373 _____. PASSING. New York: Alfred A. Knopf, 1929.

374 Lawson, William. ZEPPELIN COMING DOWN. Berkeley, Calif.: Yardbird Wing Editions, 1976.

375 Lee, Audrey. THE CLARION PEOPLE. New York: McGraw-Hill, 1968.

376 _____. THE WORKERS. New York: McGraw-Hill, 1969.

377 Lee, George Washington. RIVER GEORGE. New York: Macaulay Co., 1937.

378 Lee, James F. THE VICTIMS. New York: Vantage Press, 1959.

379 Lee, John M. COUNTER-CLOCKWISE. New York: Wendell Malliet Co., 1940.

380 Leonard, Mack. COVER MY REAR. New York: Vantage Press, 1974.

381 _____. FROM LOVE TO LOVE. Reseda, Calif.: Mojave Books, 1976.

382 _____. ANOTHER FRONT: A NOVEL OF WORLD WAR II. Reseda, Calif.: Mojave Books, 1976.

383 Lester, Julius. TWO LOVE STORIES. New York: Dial Press, 1972.
     Two novellas.

384   Lewis, Ronald. THE LAST JUNKIE. New York: Amuru, 1973.

385   Lipscomb, Ken. DUKE CASANOVA. New York: Exposition Press, 1958.

386   Liscomb, Harry F. THE PRINCE OF WASHINGTON SQUARE. New York: Frederick A. Stokes Co., 1925.

387   Love, D.C. THE SHERIFF. New York: Vantage Press, 1972.

388   Lubin, Arthur. WAMPALA ON THE HUDSON. New York: Vantage Press, 1972.

389   Lubin, Gilbert. THE PROMISED LAND. Boston: Christopher Publishing House, 1930.

390   Lucas, Curtis. FLOUR IS DUSTY. Philadelphia: Dorrance, 1943.

391   _____. THIRD WARD NEWARK. Chicago: Ziff Davis, 1946.

392   _____. SO LOW, SO LONELY. New York: Lion, 1952.

393   _____. ANGEL. New York: Lion, 1953.

394   _____. FORBIDDEN FRUIT. New York: Universal, 1953.

395   _____. LILA. New York: Lion, 1955.

396   Lyons, Charles [pseud. Is Said]. STREET JUSTICE. Columbus, Ohio: Lyons Productions, 1976.

397   McClellan, George. THE PATH OF DREAMS. Nashville, Tenn.: A.M.E. Sunday School Union, 1916.

398   McCluskey, John. LOOK WHAT THEY DONE TO MY SONG. New York: Random House, 1974.

399   McKay, Claude. HOME TO HARLEM. New York: Harper & Brothers, 1928.

400   _____. BANJO. New York: Harper & Brothers, 1929.

401 _____. BANANA BOTTOM. New York: Harper & Brothers, 1933.

402 McKenzie, William P. THE SOLEMN HOUR. New York: Carlton Press, 1972.

403 McWhortle, A.C. LENA. New York: Grove Press, 1971.

404 Mahoney, William. BLACK JACOB. New York: Macmillan, 1969.

405 Major, Clarence. ALL-NIGHT VISITORS. New York: Olympia Press, 1969.

406 _____. NO. New York: Emerson Hall, 1973.

407 _____. REFLEX AND BONE STRUCTURE. Brooklyn: Fiction Collective, 1975.

408 Mallory, Roosevelt. RADCLIFF, NO. 1: HARLEM HIT. Los Angeles: Holloway House, 1973.

409 _____. RADCLIFF, NO. 2: SAN FRANCISCO VENDETTA. Los Angeles: Holloway House, 1974.

410 _____. RADCLIFF, NO. 3: DOUBLE TROUBLE. Los Angeles: Holloway House, 1975.

411 _____. RADCLIFF, NO. 4: NEW JERSEY SHOWDOWN. Los Angeles: Holloway House, 1976.

412 Marshall, Paule. BROWN GIRL, BROWNSTONES. New York: Random House, 1959.

413 _____. THE CHOSEN PLACE, THE TIMELESS PEOPLE. New York: Harcourt, Brace & World, 1969.

414 Martin, Chester. HE WAS BORN, HE DIED AND HE LIVED. New York: Carlton Press, 1965.

415 _____. MIDDLE YEARS. New York: Carlton Press, [1965].

416 Mason, B.J. THE JERUSALEM FREEDOM MANUFACTURING CO. New York: Paperback Library, 1971.

417     Matthews, Victoria Earle. See Earle, Victoria.

418     Mayfield, Julian. THE HIT. New York: Vanguard Press, 1957.

419     _____. THE LONG NIGHT. New York: Vanguard Press, 1958.

420     _____. THE GRAND PARADE. New York: Vanguard Press, 1961.

421     Mays, James A. MERCY IS KING. Los Angeles: Crescent Publications, 1975.

422     Mays, Willie, and Jeff Harris. DANGER IN CENTER FIELD. Larchmont, N.Y.: Argonaut, 1963.

        Jeff Harris is a white author.

423     Meriwether, Louise. DADDY WAS A NUMBER RUNNER. Englewood Cliffs, N.J.: Prentice-Hall, 1970.

424     Micheaux, Oscar. THE CONQUEST. Lincoln, Nebr.: Woodruff Press, 1913.

        This is autobiographical fiction or fictional autobiography.

425     _____. THE FORGED NOTE. Lincoln, Nebr.: Western Book Supply, 1915.

426     _____. THE HOMESTEADER. Sioux City, Iowa: Western Book Supply Co., 1917.

        Essentially a new edition of THE CONQUEST (1913).

427     _____. THE WIND FROM NOWHERE. New York: Book Supply, 1941.

        Essentially a new edition of THE CONQUEST (1913).

428     _____. THE CASE OF MRS. WINGATE. New York: Book Supply, 1944.

429     _____. THE STORY OF DOROTHY STANFIELD. New York: Book Supply, 1946.

430     _____. THE MASQUERADE. New York: Book Supply, 1947.

        THE MASQUERADE is an acknowledged plagiarism of Charles W. Chesnutt's THE HOUSE BEHIND THE CEDARS (1900).

431  Middleton, Henry Davis. DREAMS OF AN IDLE HOUR. Chicago: Advocate Publishing Co., 1908.

432  Miller, Ezekiel Harry. THE PROTESTANT. Boston: Christopher Publishing House, 1933.

433  Mills, Alison. FRANCISCO. Berkeley, Calif.: Reed, Cannon and Johnson, 1974.

434  Mitchell, Loften. THE STUBBORN OLD LADY WHO RESISTED CHANGE. New York: Emerson Hall, 1973.

435  Montague, W. Reginald. OLE MAN MOSE. New York: Exposition Press, 1957.

436  Moore, Marie E. LITTLE WHITE SHOES. Hicksville, N.Y.: Exposition Press, 1975.

437  Moreau, Julian. See Jackson, J. Denis.

438  Morris, Earl J. THE COP. New York: Exposition Press, 1951.

439  Morrison, C.T. THE FLAME IN THE ICEBOX. New York: Exposition Press, 1968.

440  Morrison, Toni. THE BLUEST EYE. New York: Holt, Rinehart and Winston, 1970.

441  _____. SULA. New York: Alfred A. Knopf, 1973.

442  _____. SONG OF SOLOMON. New York: Alfred A. Knopf, 1977.

443  Motley, Willard. KNOCK ON ANY DOOR. New York: Appleton-Century, 1947.

444  _____. WE FISHED ALL NIGHT. New York: Appleton-Century-Crofts, 1951.

445  _____. LET NO MAN WRITE MY EPITAPH. New York: Random House, 1958.

446  _____. LET NOON BE FAIR. New York: G.P. Putnam's Sons, 1966.

447    Murray, Albert. TRAIN WHISTLE GUITAR. New York: McGraw-Hill, 1974.

448    Nash, T.E.D. LOVE AND VENGEANCE. Portsmouth, Va.: Privately printed, 1903.

449    Nazel, Joseph. MY NAME IS BLACK! New York: Pinnacle Books, 1973.

450    _____. THE BLACK EXORCIST. Los Angeles: Holloway House, 1974.

451    _____. BLACK IS BACK. New York: Pinnacle Books, 1974.

452    _____. THE ICEMAN, NO. 1: BILLION DOLLAR DEATH. Los Angeles: Holloway House, 1974.

453    _____. THE ICEMAN, NO. 2: THE GOLDEN SHAFT. Los Angeles: Holloway House, 1974.

454    _____. THE ICEMAN, NO. 3: SLICK REVENGE. Los Angeles: Holloway House, 1974.

455    _____. THE ICEMAN, NO. 4: SUNDAY FIX. Los Angeles: Holloway House, 1974.

456    _____. THE ICEMAN, NO. 5: SPINNING TARGET. Los Angeles: Holloway House, 1974.

457    _____. THE ICEMAN, NO. 6: CANADIAN KILL. Los Angeles: Holloway House, 1974.

458    _____. THE ICEMAN, NO. 7: THE SHAKEDOWN. Los Angeles: Holloway House, 1975.

459    _____. THE BLACK GESTAPO. Los Angeles: Holloway House, 1975.

460    _____. DEATH FOR HIRE. Los Angeles: Holloway House, 1975.

461    _____ [pseud. Dom Gober]. KILLER COP. Los Angeles: Holloway House, 1975.

462    _____. BLACK FURY. Los Angeles: Holloway House, 1976.

463       _____. BLACK PROPHET. Los Angeles: Holloway House, 1976.

464       Nelson, Annie Greene. AFTER THE STORM. Columbia, S.C.: Hampton Publishing, 1942.

465       _____. THE DAWN APPEARS. Columbia, S.C.: Hampton Publishing, 1944.

466       Newton, Leon Thomas. VERITUS, THE NIRVANA FROM THE EAST. New York: Carlton Press, 1976.

        Short fictional dialogue.

467       Offord, Carl. THE WHITE FACE. New York: Robert McBride and Co., 1943.

468       _____. THE NAKED FEAR. New York: Ace, 1951.

469       Olden, Marc. BLACK SAMURAI. New York: New American Library, 1974.

470       _____. BLACK SAMURAI, NO. 2: GOLDEN KILL. New York: New American Library, 1974.

471       _____. BLACK SAMURAI, NO. 3: KILLER WARRIOR. New York: New American Library, 1974.

472       _____. BLACK SAMURAI, NO. 4: THE DEADLY PEARL. New York: New American Library, 1974.

473       _____. BLACK SAMURAI, NO. 5: THE INQUISITION. New York: New American Library, 1974.

474       _____. BLACK SAMURAI, NO. 6: THE WARLOCK. New York: New American Library, 1975.

475       _____. BLACK SAMURAI, NO. 7: SWORD OF ALLAH. New York: New American Library, 1975.

476       _____. BLACK SAMURAI, NO. 8: THE KATANA. New York: New American Library, 1975.

477       _____. HARKER FILE, NO. 1. New York: New American Library, 1976.

478 _____. HARKER FILE, NO. 2: DEAD AND PAID FOR. New York: New American Library, 1976.

479 Ottley, Roi. WHITE MARBLE LADY. New York: Farrar, Straus & Giroux, 1965.

480 Overstreet, Cleo. THE BOAR HOG WOMAN. Garden City, N.Y.: Doubleday, 1972.

481 Palmer, Jon. HOUSE FULL OF BROTHERS. Los Angeles: Holloway House, 1973.

482 Parks, Gordon. THE LEARNING TREE. New York: Harper & Row, 1963.

483 Parrish, Clarence R. IMAGES OF DEMOCRACY. New York: Carlton Press, 1967.

484 Paulding, James E. SOMETIME TOMORROW. New York: Carlton Press, 1965.

485 Paynter, John H. FUGITIVES OF THE PEARL. Washington, D.C.: Associated Publishers, 1930.

486 Peebles, Melvin Van. See Van Peebles, Melvin.

487 Perry, Charles. PORTRAIT OF A YOUNG MAN DROWNING. New York: Simon and Schuster, 1962.

488 Perry, Richard. CHANGES. Indianapolis, Ind.: Bobbs-Merrill, 1974.

489 Petry, Ann. THE STREET. Boston: Houghton Mifflin, 1946.

490 _____. COUNTRY PLACE. Boston: Houghton Mifflin, 1947.

491 _____. THE NARROWS. Boston: Houghton Mifflin, 1953.

492 Pharr, Robert Deane. THE BOOK OF NUMBERS. Garden City, N.Y.: Doubleday, 1969.

493 _____. S.R.O. Garden City, N.Y.: Doubleday, 1971.

494 _____. THE SOUL MURDER CASE: A CONFESSION OF THE VICTIM. New York: Avon Books, 1975.

495    Phillips, Jane. MOJO HAND. New York: Trident Press, 1966.

496    Pines, Spero. See Williams, Dennis A.--joint author.

497    Pitts, Gertrude. TRAGEDIES OF LIFE. Newark, N.J.: Privately printed, 1939.

498    Polite, Carlene Hatcher. THE FLAGELLANTS. New York: Farrar, Straus & Giroux, 1967.

499    _____. SISTER X AND THE VICTIMS OF FOUL PLAY. New York: Farrar, Straus & Giroux, 1975.

500    Pollard, Freeman. SEEDS OF TURMOIL. New York: Exposition Press, 1959.

501    Potter, Valaida. SUNRISE OVER ALABAMA. New York: Comet Press, 1959.

502    Powell, Adam Clayton, Sr. PICKETING HELL. New York: Wendell Malliet Co., 1942.

503    Pretto, Clarita C. THE LIFE OF AUTUMN HOLLIDAY. New York: Exposition Press, 1958.

504    Pryor, George Langhorne. NEITHER BOND NOR FREE. New York: J.S. Ogilvie, 1902.

505    Puckett, G. Henderson. ONE MORE TOMORROW. New York: Vantage Press, 1959.

506    Ramsey, Leroy L. THE TRIAL AND THE FIRE. New York: Exposition Press, 1967.

507    Rasmussen, E.M. THE FIRST NIGHT. New York: Wendell Malliet Co., 1947.

508    Readus, James-Howard. THE DEATH MERCHANTS. Los Angeles: Holloway House, 1974.

509    _____. THE BIG HIT. Los Angeles: Holloway House, 1975.

510    _____. THE BLACK ASSASSIN. Los Angeles: Holloway House, 1975.

511 _____. BLACK RENEGADES. Los Angeles: Holloway House, 1976.

512 Redding, J. Saunders. STRANGER AND ALONE. New York: Harcourt, Brace, 1950.

513 Reed, Ishmael. THE FREE-LANCE PALLBEARERS. Garden City, N.Y.: Doubleday, 1967.

514 _____. YELLOW BACK RADIO BROKE-DOWN. Garden City, N.Y.: Doubleday, 1969.

515 _____. MUMBO JUMBO. Garden City, N.Y.: Doubleday, 1972.

516 _____. THE LAST DAYS OF LOUISIANA RED. New York: Random House, 1974.

517 _____. FLIGHT TO CANADA. New York: Random House, 1976.

518 Rhodes, Hari. A CHOSEN FEW. New York: Bantam Books, 1965.

519 Roach, Cuthbert M. See Durant, E. Elliott--joint author.

520 Roach, Thomas E. VICTOR. Boston: Meador Publishing Co., 1943.

521 _____. SAMSON. Boston: Meador Publishing Co., 1952.

522 Roberson, Sadie L. KILLER OF THE DREAM. New York: Comet, 1963.

523 Robinson, Arthur. HANG THAT NIGGER. New York: Vantage Press, 1975.

524 Robinson, J. Terry. WHITE HORSE IN HARLEM. New York: Pageant Press, 1965.

525 _____. THE DOUBLE CIRCLE PEOPLE. New York: Suzanna, 1970.

526 Robinson, Rose. EAGLE IN THE AIR. New York: Crown, 1969.

527 Rogers, J.A. FROM "SUPERMAN" TO MAN. Chicago: M.A. Donohue & Co., 1917.

> Inspirational, fictional dialogue dealing with history and sociology.

528 _____. SHE WALKS IN BEAUTY. Los Angeles: Western Publishers, 1963.

529 Rollins, Bryant. DANGER SONG. Garden City, N.Y.: Doubleday, 1967.

530 Rollins, Lamen. THE HUMAN RACE A GANG. New York: Carlton Press, 1965.

531 Rosebrough, Sadie Mae. WASTED TRAVAIL. New York: Vantage Press, 1951.

532 Ross, Fran. OREO. New York: Greyfalcon House, 1974.

533 Ross, George Hamlin. BEYOND THE RIVER: A NOVEL. Boston: Meador Publishing Co., 1938.

534 Royal, A. Bertrand. WHICH WAY TO HEAVEN? New York: Vantage Press, 1970.

535 Rudolph, Christopher. THE BOY WHO CURSED GOD. New York: Carlton Press, 1975.

536 Russ, George B. OVER EDOM, I LOST MY SHOE. New York: Carlton Press, 1970.

537 Saggittarus [sic]. See Shears, Carl L.

538 Said, Is. See Lyons, Charles.

539 Sanda. See Stowers, Walter H., and William H. Anderson.

540 Sanders, Tom. HER GOLDEN HOUR. Houston, Tex.: Privately printed, 1929.

541 Savoy, Willard W. ALIEN LAND. New York: E.P. Dutton, 1949.

542 Schuyler, George S. BLACK NO MORE. New York: Macaulay Co., 1931.

543 _____. SLAVES TODAY, A STORY OF LIBERIA. New York: Brewer, Warren and Putnam, 1931.

544   Scott, Anne. GEORGE SAMPSON BRITE. Boston: Meador Publishing Co., 1939.

545   _____. CASE 999, A CHRISTMAS STORY. Boston: Meador Publishing Co., 1953.

546   Scott-Heron, Gil. THE VULTURE. New York and Cleveland, Ohio: World, 1970.

547   _____. THE NIGGER FACTORY. New York: Dial Press, 1972.

548   Screen, Robert Martin. WE CAN'T RUN AWAY FROM HERE. New York: Vantage Press, 1958.

549   Shackelford, Otis M. LILLIAN SIMMONS. Kansas City, Mo.: R.M. Rigby, 1915.

550   Shackleford, Frank. OLD ROCKING CHAIR. New York: Vantage Press, 1975.

551   Shange, Ntozake. SASSAFRASS: A NOVELLA. San Lorenzo, Calif.: Shameless Hussy Press, 1976.

552   Shaw, Letty M. ANGEL MINK. New York: Comet, 1957.

553   Shaw, O'Wendell. GREATER NEED BELOW. Columbus, Ohio: Bi-Monthly Negro Book Club, 1936.

554   Shears, Carl L. NIGGERS AND PO' WHITE TRASH. Washington, D.C.: NuClassics and Science Publishing Co., 1971.

555   _____ [pseud. Saggittarus]. THE COUNT-DOWN TO BLACK GENOCIDE. Washington, D.C.: NuClassics and Science Publishing Co., 1973.

556   _____ [pseud. Saggittarus]. BEFORE THE SETTING SUN: THE AGE BEFORE HAMBONE. Washington, D.C.: NuClassics and Science Publishing Co., 1974.

557   Shockley, Ann Allen. LOVING HER. Indianapolis, Ind.: Bobbs-Merrill, 1974.

558   Shores, Minnie T. PUBLICANS AND SINNERS. New York: Comet Press, 1960.

559      _____. AMERICANS IN AMERICA. Boston: Christopher Publishing House, 1966.

560     Simmons, Herbert. CORNER BOY. Boston: Houghton Mifflin, 1957.

561     _____. MAN WALKING ON EGGSHELLS. Boston: Houghton Mifflin, 1962.

562     Simpson, Rawle. ADVENTURES INTO THE UNKNOWN. New York: Carlton Press, 1969.

563     Skinner, Theodosia B. ICE CREAM FROM HEAVEN. New York: Vantage Press, 1962.

564     _____. DILEMMA OF A COLLEGE GIRL. Philadelphia: Dorrance, 1972.

565     Smith, Arthur Lee. BREAK OF DAWN. Philadelphia: Dorrance, 1964.

566     Smith, Bernard S. BORN FOR MALICE. New York: Vantage Press, 1968.

567     Smith, Daniel. A WALK IN THE CITY. Cleveland, Ohio: World, 1971.

568     Smith, George Lawson. TRANSFER. New York: Vantage Press, 1970.

569     Smith, Joe. DAGMAR OF GREEN HILLS. New York: Pageant Press, 1962.

570     Smith, Lois A. [pseud. Jezebelle]. THE MOST PRECIOUS MOMENTS. Washington, D.C.: NuClassics and Science Publishing Co., 1973.

571     Smith, Maurice L. WHO CARES. New York: Carlton Press, 1968.

572     Smith, Odessa. THE FLAME. Detroit: Harlo Press, 1971.

573     Smith, Vern E. THE JONES MEN. Chicago: Henry Regnery, 1974.

574     Smith, William [psued. Will Thomas]. GOD IS FOR WHITE FOLKS. New York: Creative Age Press, 1947. Paperback Rev. and retitled LOVE KNOWS NO BARRIERS. New York: New American Library, 1950.

575     Smith, William Gardner. LAST OF THE CONQUERORS. New York: Farrar, Strauss, 1948.

576 _____. ANGER AT INNOCENCE. New York: Farrar, Straus, 1950.

577 _____. SOUTH STREET. New York: Farrar, Straus, 1954.

578 _____. THE STONE FACE. New York: Farrar, Straus, 1963.

579 Smythwick, Charles A., Jr. FALSE MEASURE. New York: William-Frederick Press, 1954.

580 Spence, Raymond. NOTHING BLACK BUT A CADILLAC. New York: G.P. Putnam's Sons, 1969.

581 Spence, Tomas H., and Eric Heath. MARTIN LARWIN. New York: Pageant Press, 1954.

582 Spencer, Mary Etta. THE RESENTMENT. Philadelphia: A.M.E. Book Concern, 1921.

583 Stampede, Herman. OF MELANCHOLY MALE. New York: Vantage Press, 1975.

584 Stewart, John. LAST COOL DAYS. London: Andre Deutsch, 1971.

585 Stone, Chuck. KING STRUT. Indianapolis, Ind.: Bobbs-Merrill, 1970.

586 Stowers, Walter H., and William H. Anderson [pseud. Sanda]. APPOINTED. Detroit: Detroit Law Printing, 1894.

587 Sublette, Walter E. [pseud. S.W. Edwards]. GO NOW IN DARKNESS. Chicago: Baker Press, 1964.

588 Sydnor, W. Leon. VERONICA. New York: Exposition Press, 1956.

589 Talbot, Dave. THE MUSICAL BRIDE. New York: Vantage Press, 1962.

590 Tarter, Charles L. FAMILY OF DESTINY. New York: Pageant Press, 1954.

591 Teague, Robert L. THE CLIMATE OF CANDOR. New York: Pageant Press, 1962.

592 Thomas, Will. See Smith, William.

593    Thorup, Lester W. CAME THE HARVEST. New York: Carlton Press, 1966.

594    Thurman, Wallace. THE BLACKER THE BERRY. New York: Macaulay Co., 1929.

595    _____. INFANTS OF THE SPRING. New York: Macaulay Co., 1932.

596    Thurman, Wallace, and A.L. Furman. THE INTERNE. New York: Macaulay Co., 1932.

       A.L. Furman is a white author.

597    Tillman, Carolyn. LIFE ON WHEELS. Los Angeles: Crescent Publications, 1975.

598    Toomer, Jean. CANE. New York: Boni and Liveright, 1923.

598A   _____. "YORK BEACH" in THE NEW AMERICAN CARAVAN. Ed. Alfred Kreymborg et al. New York: Macaulay Co., 1929.

       An extended fragment from an incomplete novel.

599    Tracy, Robert Archer. THE SWORD OF NEMESIS. New York: Neal, 1919.

600    Turner, Allen Pelzer. OAKS OF EDEN. New York: Exposition Press, 1951.

601    Turner, Peter. BLACK HEAT. New York: Belmont Books, 1970.

602    Turnor, Mae Caesar. UNCLE EZRA HOLDS PRAYER MEETING IN THE WHITE HOUSE. New York: Exposition Press, 1970.

603    Turpin, Waters Edward. THESE LOW GROUNDS. New York: Harper & Brother, 1937.

604    _____. O CANAAN! New York: Doubleday, Doran, 1939.

605    _____. THE ROOTLESS. New York: Vantage Press, 1957.

606    Underwood, Bert. A BRANCH OF VELVET. New York: Vantage Press, 1973.

# Checklist of Novels

607  Vanderpuije, Nii A. THE COUNTERFEIT CORPSE. New York: Comet, 1956.

608  Van Dyke, Henry. LADIES OF THE RACHMANINOFF EYES. New York: Farrar, Straus & Giroux, 1965.

609  _____. BLOOD OF STRAWBERRIES. New York: Farrar, Straus & Giroux, 1969.

610  _____. DEAD PIANO. New York: Farrar, Strauss & Giroux, 1971.

611  Van Peebles, Melvin. LE PERMISSION. Paris: J. Martineau, 1967.

612  _____. A BEAR FOR THE FBI. New York: Trident Press, 1968.

613  _____. SWEET SWEETBACK'S BAADASSSSS SONG. New York: Lancer, 1971.
   "Novelization" of movie script according to Van Peebles.

614  _____. DON'T PLAY US CHEAP. New York: Bantam Books, 1972.
   "Novelization" of stage musical according to Van Peebles.

615  _____. AIN'T SUPPOSED TO DIE A NATURAL DEATH. New York: Bantam Books, 1973.
   "Novelization" of stage musical according to Van Peebles.

616  _____. JUST AN OLD SWEET SONG. New York: Ballantine, Random House, 1976.
   "Novelization" of teleplay according to Van Peebles.

617  _____. THE TRUE AMERICAN: A FOLK FABLE. New York: Doubleday, 1976.

618  Vaught, Estella. VENGEANCE IS MINE. New York: Comet Press, 1959.

619  Verne, Berta. ELASTIC FINGERS. New York: Vantage Press, 1969.

620  Voglin, Peter. NOW YOU LAY ME DOWN TO SLEEP. Dallas, Tex.: Royal, 1962.

621  Walker, Alice. THE THIRD LIFE OF GRANGE COPELAND. New York: Harcourt, Brace Jovanovich, 1970.

622 _____. MERIDIAN. New York: Harcourt, Brace Jovanovich, 1976.

623 Walker, Claude, Jr. SABIH. New York: Carlton Press, 1966.

624 Walker, Drake. BUCK AND THE PREACHER. New York: Popular Books, 1971.

625 Walker, Margaret. JUBILEE. Boston: Houghton Mifflin, 1966.

626 Walker, Thomas H.B. BEBBLY, OR THE VICTORIOUS PREACHER. Gainesville, Fla.: Pepper Publishing and Printing Co., 1910.

627 _____. REVELATION, TRIAL AND EXILE OF JOHN IN EPICS. Gainesville, Fla.: Pepper Publishing and Printing Co., 1912.

628 _____. J. JOHNSON, OR THE UNKNOWN MAN. Deland, Fla.: E.O. Painter Printing, 1915.

629 Wallace, Elizabeth West. SCANDAL AT DAYBREAK. New York: Pageant Press, 1954.

630 Wamble, Thelma. ALL IN THE FAMILY. New York: New Voices, 1953.

631 _____. LOOK OVER MY SHOULDER. New York: Vantage Press, 1969.

632 Ward, Thomas Playfair. THE RIGHT TO LIVE. New York: Pageant Press, 1953.

633 _____. THE CLUTCHES OF CIRCUMSTANCES. New York: Pageant Press, 1954.

634 _____. THE TRUTH THAT MAKES MEN FREE. New York: Pageant Press, 1955.

635 Waring, Robert L. AS WE SEE IT. Washington, D.C.: C.F. Sudwarth, 1910.

636 Warner, Samuel J. MADAM PRESIDENT-ELECT. New York: Exposition Press, 1956.

637 Warren, Alyce R. INTO THESE DEPTHS. New York: Vantage Press, 1968.

638     Washington, Doris V. YULAN. New York: Carlton Press, 1964.

639     Waterman, Charles Elmer. THE WHITE FAWN: A TALE OF THE LAND OF MOLECHUNKAMUNK. Boston: Chapple Publishing Co., 1931.

640     _____. CARIB QUEENS. Boston: Bruce Humphries, 1935.

641     Watson, Lydia. See White, E.H.

642     Watson, Roberta B. CLOSED DOORS. New York: Exposition Press, 1967.

643     Webb, Charles Lewis. SASEBO DIARY. New York: Vantage Press, 1964.

644     Webb, Frank J. THE GARIES AND THEIR FRIENDS. London: G. Routledge, 1857.

645     Webster, Bill. ONE BY ONE. Garden City, N.Y.: Doubleday, 1972.

646     Wells, Jack Calvert. OUT OF THE DEEP. Boston: Christopher Publishing House, 1958.

647     Wells, Moses Peter. THREE ADVENTUROUS MEN. New York: Carlton Press, 1963.

648     West, Dorothy. THE LIVING IS EASY. Boston: Houghton Mifflin, 1948.

649     West, John B. AN EYE FOR AN EYE. New York: New American Library, 1959.

650     _____. BULLETS ARE MY BUSINESS. New York: New American Library, 1960.

651     _____. COBRA VENOM. New York: New American Library, 1960.

652     _____. A TASTE FOR BLOOD. New York: New American Library, 1960.

653     _____. DEATH ON THE ROCKS. New York: New American Library, 1961.

654 _____. NEVER KILL A COP. New York: New American Library, 1961.

655 West, William. CORNERED. New York: Carlton Press, 1964.

656 White, E.H. [pseud. Lydia Watson]. OUR HOMEWARD WAY. New York: Exposition Press, 1959.

657 White, Thomas J. TO HELL AND BACK AT 16. New York: Carlton Press, 1970.

658 White, Walter. THE FIRE IN THE FLINT. New York: Alfred A. Knopf, 1924.

649 _____. FLIGHT. New York: Alfred A. Knopf, 1926.

660 Whitney, Jim E. WAYWARD O'ER TUNER SHEFFARD. New York: Carlton Press, 1968.

661 Wideman, John Edgar. A GLANCE AWAY. New York: Harcourt, Brace & World, 1967.

662 _____. HURRY HOME. New York: Harcourt, Brace Jovanovich, 1970.

663 _____. THE LYNCHERS. New York: Harcourt, Brace Jovanovich, 1973.

664 Wiggins, Walter, Jr. DREAMS IN REALITY OF THE UNDERSEA CRAFT. New York: Pageant Press, 1954.

665 Williams, Chancellor. THE RAVEN. Philadelphia: Dorrance, 1943.

666 _____. HAVE YOU BEEN TO THE RIVER? New York: Exposition Press, 1952.

667 Williams, Dennis A., and Spero Pines. THEM THAT'S NOT. New York: Emerson Hall, 1973.

668 Williams, Edward G. NOT LIKE NIGGERS. New York: St. Martin's Press, 1969.

669 Williams, Jerome Ardell. THE TIN BOX. New York: Vantage Press, 1958.

670    Williams, John A. THE ANGRY ONES. New York: Ace, 1960; rpt. as ONE FOR NEW YORK. Chatham, N.J.: Chatham Bookseller, 1975.

671    _____. NIGHT SONG. New York: Farrar, Straus & Cudahy, 1961.

672    _____. SISSIE. New York: Farrar, Straus & Cudahy, 1963.

673    _____. THE MAN WHO CRIED I AM. Boston: Little, Brown, 1967.

674    _____. SONS OF DARKNESS, SONS OF LIGHT. Boston: Little, Brown, 1969.

675    _____. CAPTAIN BLACKMAN. Garden City, N.Y.: Doubleday, 1972.

676    _____. MOTHERSILL AND THE FOXES. Garden City, N.Y.: Doubleday, 1975.

677    _____. THE JUNIOR BACHELOR SOCIETY. Garden City, N.Y.: Doubleday, 1976.

678    Williams, Richard L. PARSON WIGGIN'S SON. New York: Carlton Press, 1964.

679    Wilson, Carl T.D. THE HALF CASTE. Ilfracombe, Eng.: Stockwell, 1964.

680    Wilson, Pat. THE SIGN OF KELOA. New York: Carlton Press, 1961.

681    Wms-Forde, Bily. REQUIEM FOR A BLACK AMERICAN CAPITALIST. New York: Troisieme Canadian, 1975.

682    Wooby, Philip. NUDE TO THE MEANING OF TOMORROW. New York: Exposition Press, 1959.

683    Wood, Lillian E. LET MY PEOPLE GO. Philadelphia: A.M.E. Book Concern, [1922].

684    Wood, Odella Phelps. HIGH GROUND. New York: Exposition Press, 1945.

685    Woods, William B. LANCASTER TRIPLE THOUSAND. New York: Exposition Press, 1956.

686    Wright, Charles. THE MESSENGER. New York: Farrar, Straus & Co., 1963.

687    _____. THE WIG, A MIRROR IMAGE. New York: Farrar, Straus & Co., 1966.

688    _____. ABSOLUTELY NOTHING TO GET ALARMED ABOUT. New York: Farrar, Straus & Giroux, 1973.

689    Wright, Richard. NATIVE SON. New York: Harper & Brothers, 1940.

690    _____. THE OUTSIDER. New York: Harper & Brothers, 1953.

691    _____. SAVAGE HOLIDAY. New York: Avon Books, 1954.

692    _____. THE LONG DREAM. Garden City, N.Y.: Doubleday, 1958.

692A    _____. "Five Episodes from an Unfinished Novel." In SOON, ONE MORNING: NEW WRITING BY AMERICAN NEGROES 1940-1962. Ed. Herbert Hill. New York: Alfred A. Knopf, 1965. Pp. 140-64.

    Excerpts from unpublished novel THE ISLAND OF HALLUCINA-TION, continuing the story of Fishbelly in THE LONG DREAM.

693    Wright, Sarah E. THIS CHILD'S GONNA LIVE. New York: Dela-corte, 1969.

694    Wright, Zara. BLACK AND WHITE TANGLED THREADS. Chicago: Privately printed, 1920.

695    _____. KENNETH. Chicago: Privately printed, 1920.

696    Wylie, James. THE LOST REBELLION. New York: Trident Press, 1971.

697    Yancey, A.H. INTERPOSITIONULIFICATION, WHAT THE NEGRO MAY EXPECT. New York: Comet, 1959.

698    Yerby, Frank. THE FOXES OF HARROW. New York: Dial Press, 1946.

699    _____. THE VIXENS. New York: Dial Press, 1947.

700 \_\_\_\_\_. THE GOLDEN HAWK. New York: Dial Press, 1948.

701 \_\_\_\_\_. PRIDE'S CASTLE. New York: Dial Press, 1949.

702 \_\_\_\_\_. FLOODTIDE. New York: Dial Press, 1950.

703 \_\_\_\_\_. A WOMAN CALLED FANCY. New York: Dial Press, 1951.

704 \_\_\_\_\_. THE SARACEN BLADE. New York: Dial Press, 1952.

705 \_\_\_\_\_. THE DEVIL'S LAUGHTER. New York: Dial Press, 1953.

706 \_\_\_\_\_. BENTON'S ROW. New York: Dial Press, 1954.

707 \_\_\_\_\_. BRIDE OF LIBERTY. Garden City, N.Y.: Doubleday, 1954.

708 \_\_\_\_\_. THE TREASURE OF PLEASANT VALLEY. New York: Dial Press, 1955.

709 \_\_\_\_\_. CAPTAIN REBEL. New York: Dial Press, 1956.

710 \_\_\_\_\_. FAIROAKS. New York: Dial Press, 1957.

711 \_\_\_\_\_. THE SERPENT AND THE STAFF. New York: Dial Press, 1958.

712 \_\_\_\_\_. JARRETT'S JADE. New York: Dial Press, 1959.

713 \_\_\_\_\_. GILLIAN. New York: Dial Press, 1960.

714 \_\_\_\_\_. THE GARFIELD HONOR. New York: Dial Press, 1961.

715 \_\_\_\_\_. GRIFFIN'S WAY. New York: Dial Press, 1962.

716 \_\_\_\_\_. THE OLD GODS LAUGH. New York: Dial Press, 1964.

717 \_\_\_\_\_. AN ODOR OF SANCTITY. New York: Dial Press, 1965.

718 \_\_\_\_\_. GOAT SONG. New York: Dial Press, 1967.

719     _____. JUDAS, MY BROTHER: THE STORY OF THE THIRTEENTH DISCIPLINE. New York: Dial Press, 1968.

720     _____. SPEAK NOW. New York: Dial Press, 1969.

721     _____. THE DAHOMEAN, AN HISTORICAL NOVEL. New York: Dial Press, 1971.

722     _____. THE GIRL FROM STORYVILLE. New York: Dial Press, 1972.

723     _____. THE VOYAGE UNPLANNED. New York: Dial Press, 1974.

724     _____. TOBIAS AND THE ANGEL. New York: Dial Press, 1975.

725     _____. A ROSE FOR ANA MARIA. New York: Dial Press, 1976.

726     Young, Al. SNAKES. New York: Holt, Rinehart and Winston, 1970.

727     _____. WHO IS ANGELINA? New York: Holt, Rinehart and Winston, 1975.

728     _____. SITTING PRETTY. New York: Holt, Rinehart and Winston, 1976.

# Chapter 2

# SHORT STORY COLLECTIONS

Included below are A. short story collections of the works of individual authors, and B. anthologies of short stories by a number of different black writers.
Each author's work is listed chronologically. Reprints are not cited, but for major reprint houses see Chapter 1, p. 1. Not included are general collections
which contain excerpts from novels, or other literary genres.

## A. COLLECTIONS OF INDIVIDUAL AUTHORS

729    Aiken, Aaron Eugene. EXPOSURE OF NEGRO SOCIETY AND SOCIE-
       TIES. . .TWENTY STORIES COMBINED. New York: J.P. Wharton
       Printer, 1916.

730    Anderson, Alston. LOVER MAN. Garden City, N.Y.: Doubleday,
       1959.

731    Anderson, Mignon Holland. MOSTLY WOMENFOLK AND A MAN OR
       TWO. Chicago: Third World Press, 1976.

732    Baldwin, James. GOING TO MEET THE MAN. New York: Dial
       Press, 1965.

733    Bambara, Toni Cade (Toni Cade). GORILLA, MY LOVE AND OTHER
       STORIES. New York: Random House, 1972.

734    Bates, Arthenia J. SEEDS BENEATH THE SNOW: VIGNETTES FROM
       THE SOUTH. New York: Greenwich Book Publishers, 1969.

735    Bohanon, Wally. WALLY BOHANON: HIS SHORT STORIES. New
       York: Amuru, 1973.

736    Bontemps, Arna. THE OLD SOUTH: "A SUMMER TRAGEDY" AND
       OTHER STORIES OF THE THIRTIES. New York: Dodd, Mead, 1973.

737    Bullins, Ed. THE HUNGERED ONE. New York: William Morrow, 1971.

738    Bullock, Clifton. BABY CHOCOLATE AND OTHER SHORT STORIES. New York: William-Frederick Press, 1975.

739    Burgess, M.L. AVE MARIA. Boston: PRESS OF THE MONTHLY REVIEW, 1895.

740    Cade, Toni. See Bambara, Toni Cade.

741    Chesnutt, Charles Waddell. THE CONJURE WOMAN. Boston: Houghton Mifflin, 1899.

742    _____. THE WIFE OF HIS YOUTH AND OTHER STORIES OF THE COLOR LINE. Boston: Houghton Mifflin, 1899.

743    _____. THE SHORT FICTION OF CHARLES W. CHESTNUTT. Ed. Sylvia Lyons Render. Washington, D.C.: Howard Univ. Press, 1974.

> Needs better documentation but has informative introduction. Does not contain all his short fiction.

744    Childress, Alice. LIKE ONE OF THE FAMILY. Brooklyn, N.Y.: Independence Publishers, 1956.

745    Colter, Cyrus. THE BEACH UMBRELLA. Iowa City: Univ. of Iowa Press, 1970.

746    Corrothers, James David. THE BLACK CAT CLUB. New York: Funk & Wagnalls, 1902.

747    Cotter, Joseph. NEGRO TALES. New York: Cosmopolitan Press, 1912.

748    Dean, Corinne. COCOANUT SUITE: STORIES OF THE WEST INDIES. Boston: Meador Publishing Co., 1944.

749    Delany, Samuel R. DRIFTGLASS. Garden City, N.Y.: Doubleday, 1971.

750    Dumas, Henry. ARK OF BONES AND OTHER STORIES. Carbondale: Southern Illinois Univ. Press, 1970.

751    Dunbar, Alice Ruth Moore (Nelson). VIOLETS AND OTHER TALES.

Boston: Privately printed, 1895.

> City and publisher are uncertain. Published under the author's maiden name, Moore.

752 _____. THE GOODNESS OF ST. ROCQUE AND OTHER STORIES. New York: Dodd, Mead, 1899.

> Published under the author's first married name, Dunbar, and sometimes listed under her second married name, Nelson.

753 Dunbar, Paul Laurence. FOLKS FROM DIXIE. New York: Dodd, Mead, 1898.

754 _____. THE STRENGTH OF GIDEON AND OTHER STORIES. New York: Dodd, Mead, 1900.

755 _____. IN OLD PLANTATION DAYS. New York: Dodd, Mead, 1903.

756 _____. THE HEART OF HAPPY HOLLOW. New York: Dodd, Mead, 1904.

757 _____. THE BEST STORIES OF PAUL LAURENCE DUNBAR. Ed. Benjamin Brawley. New York: Dodd, Mead, 1938.

758 Easterling, Renee. GIFTS FROM GOD. TWO STORIES. New York: Pageant Press, 1953.

759 Fenderson, Harold. THE PHONY AND OTHER STORIES. New York: Exposition Press, 1959.

760 Ferguson, Ira Lunan. WHICH ONE OF YOU IS INTERRACIAL? AND OTHER STORIES. San Francisco: Lunan-Ferguson Library, 1969.

761 Floyd, Silas Xavier. FLOYD'S FLOWERS. Atlanta, Ga.: Hertel, Jenkins & Co., 1905.

762 _____. SHORT STORIES FOR COLORED PEOPLE, BOTH OLD AND YOUNG. Washington, D.C.: Austin Jenkins Co., 1920.

763 _____. THE NEW FLOYD'S FLOWERS. Washington, D.C.: Austin Jenkins Co., 1922.

764 _____. CHARMING STORIES FOR YOUNG AND OLD. Washington, D.C.: Austin Jenkins Co., 1925. (Enlarged version of FLOYD'S FLOWERS).

765 Gaines, Ernest J. BLOODLINE. New York: Dial Press, 1968.

766 Garner, Carlyle W. IT WASN'T FAIR. New York: Fortuny's, 1940.

767 Groves, John Wesley, IV. PYRRHIC VICTORY: A COLLECTION OF SHORT STORIES. Philadelphia: United Publisher, 1953.

768 Herman, Jerry. AND DEATH WON'T COME: THREE SHORT STORIES. East Street, Louis, Ill.: Black River Writers, 1975.

769 Hill, Roy L. TWO WAYS AND OTHER STORIES. State College, Pa.: Commercial Printing, 1959.

770 Himes, Chester. BLACK ON BLACK: BABY SISTER AND SELECTED WRITINGS. Garden City, N.Y.: Doubleday, 1973.

771 Holder, Geoffrey, and Tom Harshman. BLACK GODS, GREEN IS-LANDS. Garden City, N.Y.: Doubleday, 1959.

Tom Harshman is a white author.

772 Howard, Wendell. THE LAST REFUGE OF A SCOUNDREL AND OTHER STORIES. New York: Exposition Press, 1952.

773 Hughes, Langston. THE WAYS OF WHITE FOLKS. New York: Alfred A. Knopf, 1934.

774 _____. SIMPLE SPEAKS HIS MIND. New York: Simon and Schuster, 1950.

775 _____. LAUGHING TO KEEP FROM CRYING. New York: Henry Holt, 1952.

776 _____. SIMPLE TAKES A WIFE. New York: Simon and Schuster, 1953.

777 _____. SIMPLE STAKES A CLAIM. New York: Rinehart, 1957.

778 _____. THE BEST OF SIMPLE. New York: Hill and Wang, 1961.

779 _____. SOMETHING IN COMMON AND OTHER STORIES. New York: Hill and Wang, 1963.

780 _____. SIMPLE'S UNCLE SAM. New York: Hill and Wang, 1965.

781 Johnson, Fenton. TALES OF DARKEST AMERICA. Chicago: Favorite Magazine, 1920.

782 Johnson, Samuel M. OFTEN BACK: THE TALES OF HARLEM. New York: Vantage Press, 1971.

783 Jones, LeRoi. TALES. New York: Grove Press, 1967.

784 Kelley, William Melvin. DANCERS ON THE SHORE. Garden City, N.Y.: Doubleday, 1964.

785 Lateef, Yusef. SPHERES. Amherst, Mass.: Fana Publishing Co., 1976.

786 Lee, George Washington. BEALE STREET SUNDOWN. New York: House of Field, 1942.

787 McClellan, George. OLD GREENBOTTOM INN AND OTHER STORIES. Louisville, Ky.: Privately printed, 1906.

788 MacDonald, Samuel E. THE OTHER GIRL, WITH SOME FURTHER STORIES AND POEMS. New York: Broadway Publishing Co., 1903.

789 McGirt, James Ephraim. THE TRIUMPHS OF EPHRAIM. Philadelphia: McGirt Publishing Co., 1907.

790 McKay, Claude. GINGERTOWN. New York: Harper & Brothers, 1932.

791 McPherson, James Alan. HUE AND CRY. Boston: Little, Brown, 1969.

792 Madden, Will Anthony. TWO AND ONE. New York: Exposition Press, 1961.

793 _____. FIVE MORE. New York: Exposition Press, 1963.

794 Marshall, Paule. SOUL CLAP HANDS AND SING. New York: Atheneum, 1961.

# Short Story Collections

795    Moore, Alice Ruth.  See Dunbar, Alice Ruth Moore [Nelson].

796    Mungin, Horace.   HOW MANY NIGGERS MAKE HALF A DOZEN.
New York: Brothers Distributing Co., 1971.

797    Nelson, Alice Ruth Moore Dunbar.  See Dunbar, Alice Ruth Moore
[Nelson].

798    Petry, Ann.  MISS MURIEL AND OTHER STORIES.  Boston: Houghton
Mifflin, 1971.

799    Pickens, William.  THE VENGEANCE OF THE GODS AND THREE
OTHER STORIES OF REAL AMERICAN COLOR LINE LIFE.  Philadelphia:
A.M.E. Book Concern, 1922.

800    _____.  AMERICAN AESOP, NEGRO AND OTHER HUMOR.  Boston:
Jordan & Moore Press, 1926.

801    Purvis, T.T.  HAGAR, THE SINGING MAIDEN, WITH OTHER STORIES
AND RHYMES.  Philadelphia: Walton & Co., 1881.

802    Stewart, John.  CURVING ROAD: STORIES.  Urbana: Univ. of Illinois Press, 1975.

803    Thornhill, Lionel O.  THE HUGE STEEL BOLT AND OTHER STORIES
AND POEMS.  New York: Vantage Press, 1966.

804    Toomer, Jean.  CANE.  New York: Boni and Liveright, 1923.
    Genre in dispute.  Listed in Chapter 1 as a novel.

805    Van Peebles, Melvin.  LE CHINOIS DU XIVe.  Paris: J. Martineau,
1966.

806    Walker, Alice.  IN LOVE AND TROUBLE: STORIES OF BLACK WO-
MEN.  New York: Harcourt, Brace Jovanovich, 1973.

807    Walrond, Eric.  TROPIC DEATH.  New York: Boni and Liveright, 1926.

808    Waterman, Charles Elmer.  THE PROMISED LAND AND OTHER TALES.
Mechanic Falls, Maine: Ledger Publishing Co., 1897.

809    Worlds, Richie.  FOUR YEARS AS A NUN AND OTHER STORIES.
New York: Carlton Press, 1969.

810   Wright, Richard. UNCLE TOM'S CHILDREN. New York: Harper & Brothers, 1938; enl. ed., 1940.

> The 1940 edition contains five stories as opposed to the 1938 edition which contains four stories. The one additional story in the 1940 edition, "Bright and Morning Star," was also published separately as a hardbound volume by International Publishers in 1941.

811   _____. EIGHT MEN. Cleveland, Ohio: World, 1961.

## B. ANTHOLOGIES

812   Adoff, Arnold, ed. BROTHERS AND SISTERS: MODERN STORIES BY BLACK AMERICANS. New York: Macmillan, 1970.

813   Bambara, Toni Cade, ed. TALES AND SHORT STORIES FOR BLACK FOLKS. Garden City, N.Y.: Doubleday, 1971.

814   Clarke, John Henrik, ed. AMERICAN NEGRO SHORT STORIES. New York: Hill and Wang, 1966.

815   _____. HARLEM: VOICES FROM THE SOUL OF BLACK AMERICA. New York: New American Library, 1970.

816   Coombs, Orde M., ed. WHAT WE MUST SEE: YOUNG BLACK STORY TELLERS. New York: Dodd, Mead, 1971.

817   Faggett, H.L. See Ford, Nick Aaron--joint editor.

818   Ford, Nick Aaron, and H.L. Faggett, eds. BEST SHORT STORIES,BY AFRO-AMERICAN WRITERS, 1925-1950. Boston: Meador Publishing Co., 1950.

819   Hughes, Langston, ed. THE BEST SHORT STORIES BY NEGRO WRITERS. Boston: Little, Brown, 1967.

820   James, Charles L., ed. FROM THE ROOTS: SHORT STORIES BY BLACK AMERICANS. New York: Dodd, Mead, 1970.

821   King, Woodie, Jr., ed. BLACK SHORT STORY ANTHOLOGY. New York: Columbia Univ. Press, 1972.

822   Mayfield, Julian, ed. TEN TIMES BLACK: STORIES FROM THE BLACK EXPERIENCE. New York: Bantam Books, 1972.

823    Mirer, Martin, ed. MODERN BLACK STORIES. New York: Barron, 1971.

824    Sanchez, Sonia, ed. WE BE WORD SORCERERS: 25 STORIES BY BLACK AMERICANS. New York: Bantam Books, 1973.

825    Stadler, Quandra Prettyman, ed. OUT OF OUR LIVES: A SELECTION OF CONTEMPORARY BLACK FICTION. Washington, D.C.: Howard Univ. Press, 1975.

826    Turner, Darwin T., ed. BLACK AMERICAN LITERATURE: FICTION. Columbus, Ohio: Charles E. Merrill, 1969.

827    Washington, Mary H., ed. BLACK-EYED SUSANS: CLASSIC STORIES BY AND ABOUT BLACK WOMEN. Garden City, N.Y.: Anchor Press, 1975.

# Chapter 3

# MAJOR AUTHORS—SECONDARY SOURCES

The following writers have been selected on the basis of generally recognized historical or literary importance. Omitted are significant authors whose primary reputation rests on grounds other than fiction, i.e., poetry, drama, or the essay. Also omitted are writers whose reputation rests almost exclusively on science fiction, historical romance, or detective fiction. Whenever feasible, the practice is to cite recent pieces that take in the largest scope of an individual author's work as well as criticism dealing with single novels and short stories. Some reprints are noted for reader reference. Authors are listed below chronologically by date of publication of first novel. Repositories of authors' manuscripts, letters, papers, and like material are listed in AMERICAN LITERARY MANUSCRIPTS (see 1087) and DIRECTORY OF AFRO-AMERICAN RESOURCES (see 1090).

## CHARLES WADDELL CHESNUTT (1858-1932)

## Bibliographies

828    Andrews, William L. "The Works of Charles W. Chesnutt: A Checklist." BB, 33 (1976), 45-47, 52.

829    _____. "Charles Waddell Chesnutt: An Essay in Bibliography." RALS, 6 (1976), 3-22.

830    Barbour, James, and Robert E. Fleming. "A Checklist of Criticism on Early Afro-American Novelists." CLAJ, 8 (1977), 21-26.

   Includes, among others, Chesnutt, pp. 22-24. For a fuller annotation, see 1052.

831    Cunningham, Joan. "Secondary Studies on the Fiction of Charles W. Chesnutt." BB, 33 (1976), 48-52.

831A    Ellison, Curtis W., and E.W. Metcalf, Jr.   CHARLES W. CHESNUTT:
        A REFERENCE GUIDE.   Boston:  G.K. Hall, 1977.

>    Lists and annotates critical commentary and reviews of
>    Chesnutt's work.   Chronologically arranged from 1887 to 1975.

832     Fisk University.   A LIST OF MANUSCRIPTS, PUBLISHED WORKS, AND
        RELATED ITEMS IN THE CHARLES WADDELL CHESNUTT COLLECTION
        OF THE ERASTUS MILO CRAVETH MEMORIAL LIBRARY.   Comp.
        Mildred Freenay and Mary T. Henry.   Nashville, Tenn.:  Fisk Univ.
        Library, 1954.

833     Keller, Dean H.   "Charles W. Chesnutt (1858-1932)."   ALR, 1 (1968),
        1-4.

>    Discussion of Chesnutt scholarship.   Contains bibliography.

834     Kirby, David K.   "Charles W. Chesnutt."   In his AMERICAN FICTION
        TO 1900:  A GUIDE TO INFORMATION SOURCES.   Detroit:  Gale
        Research Co., 1975.   Pp. 51-53.

>    Lists principal works, collected works, bibliography, biography,
>    and selected critical studies.

## Critical Studies

835     Andrews, William L.   "Chesnutt's Patesville:  The Presence and Influ-
        ence of the Past in THE HOUSE BEHIND THE CEDARS."   CLAJ, 15
        (1972), 284-94.

>    Social and moral consequences of racism.

836     _____.   "The Significance of Charles W. Chesnutt's 'Conjure Stories.'"
        SLJ, 7 (1974), 78-99.

>    They transcend regional and local color traditions.

837     _____.   "William Dean Howells and Charles W. Chesnutt:  Criticism
        and Race Fiction in the Age of Booker T. Washington."   AL, 48 (1976),
        327-39.

838     Bone, Robert A.   THE NEGRO NOVEL IN AMERICA.   Rev. ed. New
        Haven, Conn.:  Yale Univ. Press, 1965.   Pp. 35-38.

>    His short fiction is far superior to his novels.

839     _____.   "Charles Chesnutt."   In his DOWN HOME:  A HISTORY OF
        AFRO-AMERICAN SHORT FICTION FROM ITS BEGINNINGS TO THE
        END OF THE HARLEM RENAISSANCE.   New York:  G.P. Putnam's
        Sons, 1975.   Pp. 74-105.

Summary and discussion of Chesnutt's life and work.  Bone
places him in antipastoral tradition.

840   Britt, David D.  "Chesnutt's Conjure Tales:  What You See is What
You Get."  CLAJ, 15 (1972), 269-83.

Analyzes hidden structure of stories.

841   Cunningham, Joan.  "The Uncollected Short Stories of Charles Waddell
Chesnutt."  NALF, 9 (1975), 57-58.

The majority of Chesnutt's uncollected stories are about white
characters, marital conflicts, courtship, humorous family situa-
tions, and business-world encounters.

842   Dixon, Melvin.  "The Teller as Folk Trickster in Chesnutt's THE CON-
JURE WOMAN."  CLAJ, 18 (1974), 186-97.

Uncle Julius' manhood, identity, and power derive from oral
traditions.

843   Gayle, Addison, Jr.  THE WAY OF THE NEW WORLD:  THE BLACK
NOVEL IN AMERICA.  Garden City, N.Y.:  Anchor Press, Doubleday,
1975.  Pp. 47-58.

Chesnutt's ambivalent views of the mulatto, caste, and the
changing Afro-American.

844   Heermance, Noel J.  CHARLES W. CHESNUTT:  AMERICA'S FIRST
GREAT BLACK NOVELIST.  Hamden, Conn.:  Shoe String Press, 1974.

"Repeated references. . . to Chesnutt's 'greatness' are 'critically embarrassing'" (ALS 1974).

845   Reilly, John M.  "The Dilemma of Charles W. Chesnutt's THE MARROW
OF TRADITION."  PHYLON, 32 (1972), 31-38.

Irony is central to his novel and sets a precedent for subsequent Afro-American writings.

846   Wideman, John.  "Charles W. Chesnutt's THE MARROW OF TRADI-
TION."  ASch, 42 (1972), 128-34.

A close analysis of this novel.

See also 1119.

## JEAN TOOMER (1894-1967)

### Bibliographies

847    Griffin, John C.  "Jean Toomer: A Bibliography."  SCR, 7 (April 1975), 61–64.

847A   Reilly, John M.  "Jean Toomer: An Annotated Checklist of Criticism." RALS, 4 (1974), 27–56.

      Lists Toomer criticism written from 1923 to 1973.

### Critical Studies

848    Bone, Robert A.  THE NEGRO NOVEL IN AMERICA.  Rev. ed.  New Haven, Conn.: Yale Univ. Press, 1965, pp. 80–89; rpt. Durham (entry 853), pp. 58–65.

      This is an analysis of CANE, viewing part I as a southern WINESBURG, OHIO, and part II as a Washington, D.C. counterpoint.

849    _____.  "Jean Toomer."  In DOWN HOME: A HISTORY OF AFRO-AMERICAN SHORT FICTION FROM ITS BEGINNINGS TO THE END OF THE HARLEM RENAISSANCE.  New York: G.P. Putnam's Sons, 1975.  Pp. 204.

      Summary of life and works.  Contains critical examination of three stories in CANE and a discussion of post-CANE works.

850    Bontemps, Arna.  "Introduction."  CANE.  New York: Harper & Row, Perennial, 1969; rpt. Durham (entry 853), pp. 20–25.

      Toomer's life and CANE are placed in historical perspective with work of other writers by a fellow Harlem Renaissance author.

851    CLA JOURNAL, 17 (June 1974).

      Special issue on Jean Toomer.  Articles on Toomer's writing and literary influences.

852    Davis, Charles T.  "Jean Toomer and the South: Region and Race as Elements within a Literary Imagination."  SLitI, 7 (1971), 23-37.

      The relationship of geography to theme in CANE, and Toomer's artistic awareness.

853    Durham, Frank, comp. THE MERRILL STUDIES IN "CANE." Columbus, Ohio: Charles E. Merrill, 1971.

      Pieces by Waldo Frank, Arna Bontemps, W.E.B. DuBois, Saunders Redding, Hugh M. Gloster, Alain Locke, Robert A. Bone, Darwin T. Turner, Paul Rosenfeld, Gorham B. Munson, and others. No bibliography.

854    Farrison, Edward W. "Jean Toomer's CANE Again." CLAJ, 15 (1972), 295-302.

      CANE is not really a novel, not influential, and not typical of the Harlem Renaissance. It marks both the beginning and end of Toomer's success as a writer.

855    Huggins, Nathan I. HARLEM RENAISSANCE. New York: Oxford Univ. Press, 1971. Pp. 179-87.

      Toomer is the only consciously avant-garde black writer who stressed roots in the Negro's southern past.

856    Munson, Gorham. "The Significance of Jean Toomer." OPPORTUNITY, 3 (1925), 262-63; rpt. Durham (entry 853), pp. 96-100.

      An early appreciative essay by a writer who influenced him.

857    Rosenfeld, Paul. "Jean Toomer." In his MEN SEEN: TWENTY-FOUR MODERN AUTHORS. New York: Dial Press, 1925, pp. 227-33; rpt. Durham (entry 853), pp. 93-95.

858    Scruggs, Charles W. "The Mark of Cain and the Redemption of Art: A Study in Theme and Structure of Jean Toomer's CANE." AL, 44 (1972), 276-91.

      CANE may be read in terms of Cain myth, containing circular spiritual design.

859    Turner, Darwin T. "Jean Toomer: Exile." In his IN A MINOR CHORD: THREE AFRO-AMERICAN WRITERS AND THEIR SEARCH FOR IDENTITY. Carbondale: Southern Illinois Univ. Press, 1971. Pp. 1-59.

      Though organized, CANE is a collection of pieces rather than a novel. Turner also discusses other works by Toomer and relates these to his life. Many of the unpublished Toomer papers at Fisk University are succinctly described.

860    _____. "An Intersection of Paths: Correspondence Between Jean Toomer and Sherwood Anderson." CLAJ, 17 (1974), 455-67.

Some letters are partially reproduced and show the author's
diverging interests.

See also 1105, 1135, and 1164.

## ZORA NEALE HURSTON (1903-60)

## Critical Studies

861      Bone, Robert A. THE NEGRO NOVEL IN AMERICA. Rev. ed. New
Haven, Conn.: Yale Univ. Press, 1965. Pp. 126-32.

Style is more impressive than plot in Hurston's novels.

862      _____. DOWN HOME: A HISTORY OF AFRO-AMERICAN SHORT
FICTION FROM ITS BEGINNINGS TO THE END OF THE HARLEM
RENAISSANCE. New York: G.P. Putnam's Sons, 1975. Pp. 141-50.

Summary of Hurston's local-color stories and their connection
to her autobiography.

863      Gayle, Addison, Jr. THE WAY OF THE NEW WORLD: THE BLACK
NOVEL IN AMERICA. Garden City, N.Y.: Anchor Press, Doubleday,
1975. Pp. 139-50.

Hurston is closer to the Harlem Renaissance than to the new
urban revolutionary writers. Her rural characters possess dignity and are beyond stereotype.

864      Hemenway, Robert E. ZORA NEALE HURSTON: A LITERARY BIOG-
RAPHY. Urbana: Univ. of Illinois Press, 1977.

The first full-length biography. Contains a checklist of
Hurston's writings. Hemenway notes that Hurston's papers are
deposited at the Fisk University Library and the University of
South Florida Library.

865      Hurst, Fannie. "Zora Hurston: A Personality Sketch." YULG, 35
(1960), 17-22.

A brief reminiscence. Contains a checklist.

866      Hurston, Zora Neale. "What White Publishers Won't Print." NEGRO
DIGEST, 8 (April 1950), 85-89.

She deplores lack of stories about middle-class Negroes and
defends Carl Van Vechten's NIGGER HEAVEN which portrays
Negroes of wealth and culture.

867    Rayson, Ann L. "The Novels of Zora Neale Hurston." SBL, 5 (Winter 1974), 1-10.

> Hurston used folklore collected in Florida and Georgia. Rayson states: "Her novels are extended ballads."

868    Southerland, Ellease. "Zora Neale Hurston: The Novelist-Anthropologist's Life/Works." BlackW, 23 (August 1974), 20-30.

> A brief summary.

869    Turner, Darwin T. "Zora Neale Hurston: The Wandering Minstrel." In his IN A MINOR CHORD: THREE AFRO-AMERICAN WRITERS AND THEIR SEARCH FOR IDENTITY. Carbondale: Southern Illinois Univ. Press, 1971. Pp. 89-120.

> She deserves more recognition, but even her best work panders to whites. Her artistic and social judgments are "superficial and shallow."

870    Walker, Alice. "In Search of Zora Neale Hurston." MS, 3 (1975), 74-79.

> A visit to Eatonville, Florida, in search of Hurston's literary settings.

See also 1105.


# RICHARD WRIGHT (1908-60)

## Bibliographies

871    Brignano, Russell C. "Richard Wright: A Bibliography of Secondary Sources." SBL, 2.(Summer 1971), 19-25.

872    Bryer, Jackson R. "Richard Wright (1908-1960): A Selected Checklist of Criticism." WSCL, 1 (Fall 1960), 22-33.

873    Corrigan, Robert A., comp. RICHARD WRIGHT AND HIS INFLUENCE. Iowa City: Univ. of Iowa, 1971.

> The first of two volumes were prepared and distributed in a limited number of copies to conferees of the Third Annual Institute for Afro-American Culture, July 1971. Most chapters do not relate directly to Wright but to the widest scope of the literary culture.

874    Corrigan, Robert A., and Donald B. Gibson, comps. RICHARD
       WRIGHT'S FICTION: THE CRITICAL RESPONSE 1940-1971. Iowa City:
       Univ. of Iowa, 1971.

       This is the second of two volumes noted above. Includes
       secondary sources, 62 essays and reviews about Wright's work,
       reproduced for participants of the Third Annual Institute for
       Afro-American Culture, July 1971.

875    Fabre, Michel, and Edward Margolies. "Richard Wright (1908-1960):
       A Bibliography." BB, 24 (1965), 131-33, 137; rpt. Webb (entry 904),
       1968, 423-29; rpt. NEGRO DIGEST, 18 (January 1969), 86-92; rpt.
       NewL (entry 898), revised bibliography; rpt. Ray and Farnsworth (entry
       899), 1973, 191-205; rpt. Fabre (entry 892), 1973, 625-38.

876    Gibson, Donald B. "Richard Wright: A Bibliographical Essay." CLAJ,
       12 (1969), 360-65.

       Gibson focuses on major critical material, superseded by
       John M. Reilly (entry 879).

877    _____. "Bibliography: Richard Wright." In his FIVE BLACK WRITERS:
       ESSAYS ON WRIGHT, ELLISON, BALDWIN, HUGHES, AND LEROI
       JONES. New York: New York Univ. Press, 1970. Pp. 303-05.

       Good selection of secondary sources.

878    Kinnamon, Keneth, and Joseph Benson. RICHARD WRIGHT: AN IN-
       TERNATIONAL BIBLIOGRAPHY. Boston: G.K. Hall, in progress.

879    Reilly, John M. "Richard Wright: An Essay In Bibliography." RALS,
       1 (1971), 131-90.

       Updated by Reilly in BLACK AMERICAN WRITERS. Vol. 2,
       pp. 1-46 (see entry 1071). Excellent annotated survey of
       scholarship and criticism.

880    THE RICHARD WRIGHT ARCHIVE. Beinecke Library, Yale University,
       to be published.

881    Sprague, M.D. "Richard Wright: A Bibliography." BB, 21 (1953),
       39.

       The first bibliography, subsequently superseded by Fabre and
       Margolies (entry 875).

## Critical Studies

882    Abcarian, Richard, ed. RICHARD WRIGHT'S "NATIVE SON": A
       CRITICAL HANDBOOK. Belmont, Calif.: Wadsworth, 1970.

Essays by and about Wright's NATIVE SON. Also contains a chronology of Wright's life and a selected bibliography of secondary sources.

883    Baker, Houston A., Jr., ed. TWENTIETH CENTURY INTERPRETATIONS OF "NATIVE SON." Englewood Cliffs, N.J.: Prentice-Hall, 1972.

Reprints pieces by Richard Wright, James Baldwin, Irving Howe, Robert A. Bone, George E. Kent, Donald B. Gibson, and others.

884    Bakish, David. "Underground in an Ambiguous Dreamworld." SBL, 2 (Autumn 1971), 18-23.

An examination of images and symbols in "The Man Who Lived Underground."

885    _____. RICHARD WRIGHT. New York: Frederick Ungar, 1973.

Monograph on life and works.

886    Baldwin, James. "Everybody's Protest Novel." ZERO (France), No. 1 (Spring 1949), 54-58; rpt. PR, 16 (1949), 578-85; rpt. in his NOTES OF A NATIVE SON. Boston: Beacon Press, 1955. Pp. 13-23.

NATIVE SON marred by sociological vision.

887    _____. "Many Thousands Gone." PR, 17 (1951), 665-80; rpt. in his NOTES OF A NATIVE SON. Boston: Beacon Press, 1955. Pp. 24-45.

Continues attack on Wright that began with "Everybody's Protest Novel," above.

888    Bone, Robert A. RICHARD WRIGHT. Minneapolis: Univ. of Minnesota Press, 1969.

A monograph.

889    Brignano, Russell Carl. RICHARD WRIGHT: AN INTRODUCTION TO THE MAN AND HIS WORKS. Pittsburgh: Univ. of Pittsburgh Press, 1970.

Emphasizes race relations in the United States, Marxism, and new perspective from outside America.

890    CLA JOURNAL, 12 (June 1969).

Special issue on Richard Wright. Articles by Blyden Jackson, Darwin T. Turner, George E. Kent, Donald B. Gibson, and Keneth Kinnamon.

891    Fabre, Michel. "Richard Wright: The Man Who Lived Underground."
       SNNTS, 3 (1971), 165-79.

       Tracks down American sources of the novella.

892    _____. THE UNFINISHED QUEST OF RICHARD WRIGHT. New York:
       William Morrow, 1973.

       A thorough study of Wright's life and work. Deals with much
       unpublished material.

892 A  Fishburn, Katherine. RICHARD WRIGHT'S HERO: THE FACES OF A
       REBEL-VICTIM. Metuchen, N.J.: Scarecrow Press, 1977.

       Deals with Wright's heroes from an existentialist point of view.

893    Kinnamon, Keneth. THE EMERGENCE OF RICHARD WRIGHT: A
       STUDY IN LITERATURE AND SOCIETY. Urbana: Univ. of Illinois
       Press, 1972.

       Much emphasis on early poetry and Chicago and Mississippi
       background. Good bibliography.

894    McCall, Dan. THE EXAMPLE OF RICHARD WRIGHT. New York:
       Harcourt, Brace, & World, 1969.

       One of the first popular biographies.

895    Margolies, Edward. "Richard Wright: NATIVE SON and Three Kinds
       of Revolution." In his NATIVE SONS: A CRITICAL STUDY OF
       TWENTIETH-CENTURY NEGRO AMERICAN AUTHORS. Philadelphia:
       Lippincott, 1968. Pp. 65-86.

       NATIVE SON, a powerful work but conflicting ideologies de-
       tract somewhat from its effectiveness.

896    _____. THE ART OF RICHARD WRIGHT. Carbondale: Southern Illi-
       nois Univ. Press, 1969.

       A critical examination of all of Wright's published prose works.

897    NEGRO DIGEST, 18 (December 1968).

       Special issue on Richard Wright. Articles by Addison Gayle,
       Jr., James A. Emanuel, John A. Williams, Faith Berry, Cecil
       M. Brown, Ronald Sanders, and Horace Cayton. Also a photo
       feature on Wright, with thirteen photographs, and a reprinting
       of "Bright and Morning Star."

898    NEW LETTERS, 38 (Winter 1971).

Special issue on the life and work of Richard Wright, including
his haiku and some previously unpublished prose. Pieces by
Edward A. Watson, Katherine Sprandel, and Morris Dickstein
deal with Wright's fiction. Contains also an updated Wright
bibliography by Michel Fabre and Edward Margolies.

899    Ray, David, and Robert M. Farnsworth, eds. RICHARD WRIGHT: IM-
PRESSIONS AND PERSPECTIVES. Ann Arbor: Univ. of Michigan Press,
1973.

Basically a reissue of NEW LETTERS' special issue on Wright,
above.

900    Reilly, John M., ed. RICHARD WRIGHT: THE CRITICAL RECEPTION.
New York: Burt Franklin, 1978.

A superb selection of newspaper and magazine reviews of all
Wright's works. Reilly gives an excellent overview in his
introduction, pp. ix–xli.

901    Rickels, Milton, and Patricia Rickels. RICHARD WRIGHT. Austin,
Tex.: Steck-Vaugn, 1970.

Pamphlet. Analysis of Wright's imagery as outgrowth of
southern black folk culture.

902    Scott, Nathan A. "The Dark and Haunted Tower of Richard Wright."
GRADUATE COMMENT (Wayne State University), 7 (July 1964), 93–
99; rpt. in BLACK EXPRESSION: ESSAYS BY AND ABOUT BLACK
AMERICANS IN THE CREATIVE ARTS. Ed. Addison Gayle, Jr.
New York: Weybright and Talley, 1969, pp. 296–311; rpt. in THE
BLACK NOVELIST. Ed. Robert Hemenway. Columbus, Ohio:
Charles E. Merrill, 1970, pp. 72–87; rpt. in FIVE BLACK WRITERS:
ESSAYS ON WRIGHT, ELLISON, BALDWIN, HUGHES, AND LEROI
JONES. Ed. Donald B. Gibson. New York: New York Univ. Press,
1970. Pp. 12–25.

Wright's existentialism is a partially unconscious outgrowth of
southern racism.

903    Sillen, Samuel. "The Meaning of Bigger Thomas." NEW MASSES, 35
(1960), 13–21.

A Communist Party view, stressing social responsibility. A
Marxist understanding of character development.

904    Webb, Constance. RICHARD WRIGHT: A BIOGRAPHY. New York:
G.P. Putnam's Sons, 1968.

The first full-length biography. Deals with much unpublished material.

905     Widmer, Kingsley. "The Existential Darkness: Richard Wright's THE OUTSIDER." WSCL, 1 (Fall 1960), 13-21; rpt. in FIVE BLACK WRITERS: ESSAYS ON WRIGHT, ELLISON, BALDWIN, HUGHES, AND LEROI JONES. Ed. Donald B. Gibson. New York: New York Univ. Press, 1970, pp. 50-57; rpt., rev. version, in MODERN BLACK NOVELISTS: A COLLECTION OF CRITICAL ESSAYS. Ed. M.G. Cooke, Englewood Cliffs, N.J.: Prentice-Hall, 1971. Pp. 79-87.

"One of the very few consciously existential works in American literature." THE OUTSIDER is worthy of more positive critical response.

905A    Wright, Richard. "Five Episodes from an Unfinished Novel." In SOON, ONE MORNING: NEW WRITING BY AMERICAN NEGROES 1940-1962. Ed. Herbert Hill. New York: Alfred A. Knopf, 1965. Pp. 140-64.

Excerpts from the unpublished novel, THE ISLAND OF HALLUCI-NATION, continuing the story of Fishbelly in THE LONG DREAM.

See also 1118, 1129, 1130, 1135, and 1164.

## CHESTER HIMES (1909-  )

## Bibliographies

906     Fabre, Michel. "A Selected Bibliography of Chester Himes' Work." BlackW, 21 (March 1972), 76-78.

907     Hill, James Lee. "Bibliography of the Works of Chester Himes, Ann Petry, and Frank Yerby." BLACK BOOKS BULLETIN, 3 (1975), 60-72.

## Critical Studies

908     Bakish, David. "Chester Himes." ENCYCLOPEDIA OF WORLD LITERA-TURE IN THE 20TH CENTURY. Vol. 4. New York: Frederick Ungar, 1975.

909     BLACK WORLD, 21 (March 1972).

Special issue on Chester Himes. Contains articles by Hoyt W. Fuller, Ishmael Reed, and Michel Fabre.

910     Fuller, Hoyt. "Traveller on the Long, Rough, Lonely Old Road: An Interview with Chester Himes." BlackW, 21 (March 1972), 4-22, 87-98.

911 Himes, Chester. "Reading Your Own." NYTBR, 4 June 1967, p. 7.

Says THE PRIMITIVE is his favorite novel.

912 _____. THE QUALITY OF HURT: THE AUTOBIOGRAPHY OF CHESTER HIMES. Vol. I. Garden City, N.Y.: Doubleday, 1973.

Makes occasional allusions to his fiction.

913 MY LIFE OF ABSURDITY: THE AUTOBIOGRAPHY OF CHESTER HIMES. Vol. II. Garden City, N.Y.: Doubleday, 1976.

Makes occasional allusions to his fiction.

914 Lundquist, James. CHESTER HIMES. New York: Frederick Ungar, 1976.

Short general survey of life and works.

915 Margolies, Edward. "Race and Sex: The Novels of Chester Himes." In his NATIVE SONS: A CRITICAL STUDY OF TWENTIETH–CENTURY NEGRO AMERICAN AUTHORS. Philadelphia: Lippincott, 1968. Pp. 87-101.

General critical survey with emphasis on THE PRIMITIVE.

916 _____. "The Thrillers of Chester Himes." SBL, 1 (Summer 1970), 1-11.

Discusses Himes's use of hard-boiled genre in Harlem novels.

917 _____. "Experiences of the Black Expatriate Writer: Chester Himes." CLAJ, 15 (1972), 421-27.

Based on Himes's correspondence and a novel Himes wrote about black intellectuals in France (UNE AFFAIRE DE VIOL, 1963), not yet published in English.

918 Micha, Rene. "Les Paroissiens de Chester Himes." TEMPS MODERNES, 20 (1965), 1507-23.

Himes is likened to Dickens in his treatment of the poor.

919 Milliken, Stephen F. CHESTER HIMES: A CRITICAL APPRAISAL. Columbia: Univ. of Missouri Press, 1976.

Himes is a major neglected author.

920 Nelson, Raymond. "Domestic Harlem: The Detective Fiction of Chester Himes." VQR, 48 (1972), 260-76.

Harlem as a surreal metaphor for America.

921    Williams, John A.  "My Man Himes:  An Interview with Chester Himes."
       In AMISTAD 1.  Ed. John A. Williams and Charles F. Harris.  New
       York: Vintage Books, 1970.  Pp. 25-91.  Rpt. in his FLASHBACKS:
       A TWENTY-YEAR DIARY OF ARTICLE WRITING.  Garden City, N.Y.:
       Anchor Press, Doubleday, 1973.  Pp. 292-352.

922    _____.  "Chester Himes is Getting On."  NYHTBW, 11 October
       1964, pp. 2, 21.

       Williams discusses Himes's fiction, a screenplay, and life views.

## ANN PETRY (1911-  )

## Bibliographies

923    Hill, James Lee.  "Bibliography of the Works of Chester Himes, Ann Petry,
       and Frank Yerby."  BLACK BOOKS BULLETIN, 3 (Fall 1975), 60-72.

## Critical Studies

924    Adams, George R.  "Riot as Ritual: Ann Petry's 'In Darkness and Con-
       fusion.'"  NALF, 6 (1972), 54-57, 60.

       Petry's story transforms aspects of 1943 Harlem riot into artistic
       expression.

925    "Ann Petry."  In INTERVIEWS WITH BLACK WRITERS.  Ed. John
       O'Brien.  New York: Liveright, 1973, pp. 153-63.

926    Bone, Robert A.  THE NEGRO NOVEL IN AMERICA.  Rev. ed.  New
       Haven, Conn.: Yale Univ. Press, 1965.  Pp. 180-85.

       COUNTRY PLACE is assimilationism and comparable in some
       ways to the works of Sinclair Lewis.  THE STREET belongs to
       Richard Wright's school of naturalism.

927    Gayle, Addison, Jr.  THE WAY OF THE NEW WORLD: THE BLACK
       NOVEL IN AMERICA.  Garden City, N.Y.: Anchor Press, Doubleday,
       1975.  Pp. 191-97.

       THE STREET is a major breakthrough in realistic portrayal of
       urban life.  Petry is a good stylist and delineator of characters.

928    Ivy, James W.  "Ann Petry Talks About Her First Novel."  CRISIS, 53
       (1946), 43-46.

929    _____.  "Mrs. Petry's Harlem."  CRISIS, 53 (1946), 48-49.

930    Littlejohn, David. BLACK ON WHITE: A CRITICAL SURVEY OF WRIT-
       ING BY AMERICAN NEGROES. New York: Grossman, 1966.
       Pp. 154-56.

> Her plots are contrived and sordid, but her intelligence and
> style are impressive.

931    Morris, Wright. "The Complexity of Evil." NY TIMES, 16 August
       1953, p. 4.

> In THE NARROWS she successfully links past to present, but her
> treatment of the present is unrealistic.

932    Shinn, Thelma J. "Women in the Novels of Ann Petry." Crit, 16,
       no. 1 (1974), 110-20.

> Rebellious heroines often become an expression of the society
> that oppresses them. Inequities rob weak and strong alike.

933    Trilling, Diana. "Class and Color." NATION, 162 (9 March 1946),
       290.

> THE NARROWS examines social class in black and white com-
> munities.

## WILLIAM DEMBY (1922-  )

## Critical Studies

934    Bone, Robert A. THE NEGRO NOVEL IN AMERICA. Rev. ed. New
       Haven, Conn.: Yale Univ. Press, 1965. Pp. 191-96.

> BEETLECREEK "is an existentialist novel. . .dominated by pes-
> simism and disgust flowing from a robust rejection of American
> culture and Negro life in particular."

935    _____. "William Demby's Dance of Life." TriQ, 15 (Spring 1969),
       127-41.

> THE CATACOMBS has an attenuated plot line with exception-
> ally rich thematic structure; it probes the outer limits of con-
> temporary consciousness.

936    Cayton, Horace. Rev. of BEETLECREEK, by William Demby. NY
       TIMES, 26 February 1950, p. 4.

> Lacks central focus but deals admirably with black-white re-
> lationships in small backwater southern town.

937    Connelly, Joseph F.  "William Demby's Fiction:  The Pursuit of Muse."
       NALF, 10 (1976), 100, 102-3.

       THE CATACOMBS is a documentary of an important part of
       Demby's life.

938    Conroy, Jack.  Rev. of BEETLECREEK, by William Demby.  CHICAGO
       SUN, 23 March 1950, p. 6.

       A curious reluctance to grasp essentially dramatic material
       mars an otherwise effective book.

939    Fuller, Edmund.  Rev. of BEETLECREEK, by William Demby.  Sat. R.
       of Lit., 4 March 1950, p. 17.

       Succeeds in conveying "delicate and difficult relationships
       and has strength and range beyond this single aspect."

940    Hoffman, Nancy Y.  "Technique in Demby's THE CATACOMBS."  SBL,
       2 (Summer 1971), 10-13.

       Avant-garde experiments blur reality and fantasy.  Likens
       Demby to Borges, Nabokov, Teilhard, and McLuhan.

940A    _____.  "The Annunciation of William Demby."  SBL, 3 (Spring 1972),
       8-13.

       The black artist is a symbol of human redemption in THE
       CATACOMBS.

941    Johnson, Joe.  "Interview with William Demby."  BLACK CREATION,
       3 (Spring 1972), 18-21.

942    Margolies, Edward.  "The Expatriate as Novelist:  William Demby."
       In his NATIVE SONS: A CRITICAL STUDY OF TWENTIETH CENTURY
       NEGRO AUTHORS. Philadelphia: J.B. Lippincott, 1968. Pp. 173-89.

       THE CATACOMBS is an acceptance of western civilization
       despite protagonist's racial hurts.

943    "William Demby."  SBL, 3 (Fall 1972), 1-6; rpt. in INTERVIEWS WITH
       BLACK WRITERS.  Ed. John O'Brien.  New York: Liveright, 1973.
       Pp. 35-53.

## RALPH ELLISON (1914-  )

## Bibliographies

944    Baily, Lugene, and Frank E. Moorer.  "A Selected Checklist of Mate-

rial By and About Ralph Ellison."  BlackW, 20 (December 1970), 126-30.

945  Benoit, Bernard, and Michel Fabre.  "A Bibliography of Ralph Ellison's Published Writings."  SBL, 2 (Autumn 1971), 25-28.

945A  Covo, Jacqueline.  "Ralph Waldo Ellison:  Bibliographic Essays and Finding List of American Criticism, 1952-1964."  CLAJ, 15 (1971), 171-96.

946  _____.  "Ralph Ellison in France:  Bibliographic Essays and Checklist of French Criticism, 1954-1971."  CLAJ, 16 (1973), 519-26.

947  _____.  THE BLINKING EYE:  RALPH WALDO ELLISON AND HIS AMERICAN, FRENCH, GERMAN AND ITALIAN CRITICS, 1952-1971. Metuchen, N.J.:  Scarecrow Press, 1974.

> Checklists and assessment of critical response to Ellison ar-ranged by individual country.  Includes updated material originally in CLAJ (see 945A and 946).

948  Gibson, Donald B.  "Bibliography:  Ralph Ellison."  In his FIVE BLACK WRITERS:  ESSAYS ON WRIGHT, ELLISON, BALDWIN, HUGHES, AND LEROI JONES.  New York:  New York Univ. Press, 1970.  Pp. 305-6.

> Good selection of secondary sources.

## Critical Studies

949  BLACK WORLD, 20 (December 1970).

> Special issue on Ralph Ellison, with articles by Nick Aaron Ford, John A. Williams, Eugenia W. Collier, Clifford Mason, John Henrik Clarke, Larry Neal, Ernest Kaiser, and John Corry.  Checklist by Lugene Baily and Frank E. Moorer (see entry 944).

949A  Chester, Alfred, and Vilma Howard.  "The Art of Fiction:  An Interview." PARIS REVIEW, 3 (Spring 1955), 55-71; rpt. in WRITERS AT WORK: THE PARIS REVIEW INTERVIEWS, 2nd ser.  Ed. George Plimpton.  New York:  Viking Press, 1963, pp. 317-34; rpt. in Ellison's SHADOW AND ACT.  New York:  Random House, 1964.  Pp. 167-83.

> Famous interview in which Ellison discusses INVISIBLE MAN.

950  CLA JOURNAL, 13 (March 1970).

> Special issue on Ralph Ellison.  Articles by Archie D. Sanders,

Lawrence J. Clipper, Eleanor R. Wilner, Darwin T. Turner, George E. Kent, Phyllis R. Klotman, Lloyd W. Brown, Floyd R. Horowitz, and Thomas LeClair.

951    Doyle, Mary Ellen. "In Need of Folk: The Alienated Protagonists of Ralph Ellison's Short Fiction." CLAJ, 19 (1975), 165-72.

The protagonists of Ellison's short stories resolve their alienation by perceiving their links to Negro past and folk culture.

952    Ellison, Ralph. "The World and the Jug" and "A Rejoinder." THE NEW LEADER, 46 (9 December 1963), 22-26, and 47 (3 February 1964), 15-22; rpt. in his SHADOW AND ACT. New York: Random House, 1964, pp. 107-20 and 120-43; rpt. in FIVE BLACK WRITERS: ESSAYS ON WRIGHT, ELLISON, BALDWIN, HUGHES, AND LEROI JONES. New York: New York Univ. Press, 1970, pp. 271-95; rpt. in A CASEBOOK ON RALPH ELLISON'S "INVISIBLE MAN." Ed. Joseph F. Trimmer. New York: Thomas Y. Crowell, 1972. Pp. 171-200.

Ellison responds to Irving Howe's views on his debt to Richard Wright.

953    Gayle, Addison, Jr. THE WAY OF THE NEW WORLD: THE BLACK NOVEL IN AMERICA. Garden City, N.Y.: Anchor Press, Doubleday, 1975. Pp. 204-15.

Although rich in projecting black life, INVISIBLE MAN is flawed by protagonist choosing individualism rather than racial unity.

953A    Gottesman, Ronald. STUDIES IN "INVISIBLE MAN." Columbus, Ohio: Charles E. Merrill, 1971.

Seven previously published essays and the well-known PARIS REVIEW interview with Ellison (see entry 949A).

954    Hersey, John, ed. RALPH ELLISON: A COLLECTION OF CRITICAL ESSAYS. Englewood Cliffs, N.J.: Prentice-Hall, 1974.

Essays by George E. Kent, Larry Neal, Robert Penn Warren, James A. McPherson, Saul Bellow, Irving Howe, Stanley E. Hyman, and others. Bibliography.

955    Howe, Irving. "Black Boys and Native Sons." DISSENT, 10 (1963), 353-68; rpt. in his A WORLD MORE ATTRACTIVE: A VIEW OF MODERN LITERATURE AND POLITICS. New York: Horizon Press, 1963, pp. 98-122; rpt. in A CASEBOOK ON RALPH ELLISON'S "INVISIBLE MAN." Ed. Joseph F. Trimmer. New York: Thomas Y. Crowell, 1972. Pp. 150-69.

Richard Wright's rage and rebellion in NATIVE SON have liberated authors like Ralph Ellison and James Baldwin despite their denials.

956    "Ralph Ellison." In INTERVIEWS WITH BLACK WRITERS. Ed. John O'Brien. New York: Liveright, 1973. Pp. 63-77.

957    Reilly, John M., ed. TWENTIETH CENTURY INTERPRETATIONS OF "INVISIBLE MAN." Englewood Cliffs, N.J.: Prentice-Hall, 1970.

Includes reprints of critics' interpretations and viewpoints; comments by Robert Bone, Charles I. Glicksberg, Earl H. Rovit, Esther Merle Jackson, Therman B. O'Daniel, Irving Howe, and others.

958    Rovit, Earl H. "Ralph Ellison and The American Comic Tradition." WSCL, 1 (Fall 1960), 34-42; rpt. in RECENT AMERICAN FICTION: SOME CRITICAL VIEWS. Ed. Joseph J. Waldmeir. Boston: Houghton Mifflin, 1963, pp. 167-74; rpt. in FIVE BLACK WRITERS: ESSAYS ON WRIGHT, ELLISON, BALDWIN, HUGHES, AND LEROI JONES. Ed. Donald B. Gibson. New York: New York Univ. Press, 1970, pp. 108-15; rpt. in TWENTIETH CENTURY INTERPRETATIONS OF "INVISIBLE MAN." Ed. John M. Reilly. Englewood Cliffs, N.J.: Prentice-Hall, 1970, pp. 56-63; rpt. in RALPH ELLISON: A COLLECTION OF CRITICAL ESSAYS. Ed. John Hersey. Englewood Cliffs, N.J.: Prentice-Hall, 1974. Pp. 151-59.

INVISIBLE MAN falls into larger contours of American comic tradition.

959    Trimmer, Joseph F., ed. A CASEBOOK ON RALPH ELLISON'S "IN-VISIBLE MAN." New York: Thomas Y. Crowell, 1972.

Essays and articles on historical background, an exchange of views by Irving Howe and Ellison, critical pieces by Bone, Rovit, and others. A good bibliography.

960    Walling, William. "'Art' and 'Protest': Ralph Ellison's INVISIBLE MAN Twenty Years After." PHYLON, 34 (1973), 120-34.

A consideration of Ellison's novel in an "American society which has experienced a radical alteration in black conscious-ness." Despite a variety of attacks, the novel continues to stand up aesthetically and may well be a classic.

See also 1118, 1119, 1129, 1130, and 1135.

## JAMES BALDWIN (1924- )

### Bibliographies

961    Fischer, Russell G. "James Baldwin: A Bibliography, 1947-1962." BB, 24 (1965), 127-30.

962    Gibson, Donald B. "Bibliography: James Baldwin." In his FIVE BLACK WRITERS: ESSAYS ON WRIGHT, ELLISON, BALDWIN, HUGHES, AND LEROI JONES. New York: New York Univ. Press, 1970. Pp. 306-8.

    Good selection of secondary sources.

963    Kindt, Kathleen A. "James Baldwin: A Checklist, 1947-62." BB, 24 (1965), 123-26.

964    O'Daniel, Therman B. "James Baldwin: A Classified Bibliography." In his JAMES BALDWIN: A CRITICAL EVALUATION. Washington, D.C.: Howard Univ. Press, 1977. Pp. 243-61.

965    Standley, Fred L. "James Baldwin: A Checklist, 1963-1967." BB, 25 (1968), 135-37, 160.

### Critical Studies

966    Bone, Robert [A.]. "James Baldwin." In his THE NEGRO NOVEL IN AMERICA. Rev. ed. New Haven, Conn.: Yale Univ. Press, 1965. Pp. 215-39.

    Baldwin is strongest as essayist, weakest as playwright, and successful in only one novel, GO TELL IT ON THE MOUN-TAIN, an impressive achievement.

967    Cleaver, Eldridge. "Notes on a Native Son." RAMPARTS, June 1966, pp. 51-56; rpt. in his SOUL ON ICE. New York: McGraw-Hill, 1968, pp. 97-111; rpt. in JAMES BALDWIN: A COLLECTION OF CRITICAL ESSAYS. Ed. Keneth Kinnamon. Englewood Cliffs, N.J.: Prentice-Hall, 1974. Pp. 66-76.

    Baldwin's writings are filled with racial self-hatred. His attack on Richard Wright stems from homosexual fears of masculinity.

968    Eckman, Fern Marja. THE FURIOUS PASSAGE OF JAMES BALDWIN. New York: M. Evans, 1966.

    A popular biography by a journalist.

969    Gayle, Addison Jr. THE WAY OF THE NEW WORLD: THE BLACK
       NOVEL IN AMERICA. Garden City, N.Y.: Anchor Press, Doubleday,
       1975. Pp. 213-20.

      Baldwin is an integrationist at heart bewailing the fact that
       whites don't accept him. This is especially apparent in
       ANOTHER COUNTRY.

970    Kinnamon, Keneth, ed. JAMES BALDWIN: A COLLECTION OF
       CRITICAL ESSAYS. Englewood Cliffs, N.J.: Prentice-Hall, 1974.

      Reprinted pieces by George E. Kent, Robert A. Bone, Eldridge
       Cleaver, Irving Howe, Calvin C. Hernton, Michel Fabre,
       John M. Reilly, and others.

971    Macebuh, Stanley. JAMES BALDWIN: A CRITICAL STUDY. New
       York: Third Press, 1973.

      A Nigerian critic's view of Baldwin's philosophy and literary
       technique.

972    O'Daniel, Therman B., ed. JAMES BALDWIN: A CRITICAL EVALU-
       ATION. Washington, D.C.: Howard Univ. Press, 1977.

      Essays on Baldwin's fiction by Donald B. Gibson, George E.
       Kent, Jacqueline E. Orsagh, William Edward Farrison, John
       M. Reilly, Arthenia Bates Millican, and others. Extensive
       bibliography and notes.

973    Williams, Sherley Anne. GIVE BIRTH TO BRIGHTNESS: A THEMATIC
       STORY IN NEO-BLACK LITERATURE. New York: Dial Press, 1972.

      According to ALS (entry 1050) this book is "shaggy." It is
       topical, with emphasis on Baraka, Baldwin, and Gaines, and
       contains no index.

      See also 1118, 1119, 1129, 1130, and 1164.

## PAULE MARSHALL (1929-  )

## Critical Studies

974    Benston, Kimberly. "Architectural Imagery and Unity in Paule Marshall's
       BROWN GIRL, BROWNSTONES." NALF, 9 (Fall 1975), 67-70.

      Unity is achieved through a sustained imagery. The dominant
       trope is architectural, binding work's moral and existential
       antinomies.

975     Bone, Robert [A.]. Rev. of THE CHOSEN PLACE, THE TIMELESS PEOPLE, by Paule Marshall. NYTBR, 30 November 1969, p. 4.

> "One of the four or five most impressive novels ever written by a black American." Transforms politics and history into ritual and myth.

976     Braithwaite, Edward. "West Indian History and Society in the Art of Paule Marshall's Novel." JOURNAL OF BLACK STUDIES, 1 (1970), 225-38.

> CHOSEN PLACE shows development springs from discovery of self and the history of one's people.

977     Brown, Lloyd W. "The Rhythms of Power in Paule Marshall's Fiction." NOVEL, 7 (1974), 159-67.

> Rhythms and structures project ethnic and feminist themes.

978     Giddings, Paula. "A Special Vision, a Common Goal." ENCORE AMERICAN AND WORLDWIDE NEWS, 23 June 1975, 44-48.

> Cultural conflicts activate her characters.

979     Kapai, Leela. "Dominant Themes and Technique in Paule Marshall's Fiction." CLAJ, 16 (1972), 49-59.

> Emphasis is on SOUL CLAP HANDS AND SING.

980     Keizs, Marcia. "Themes and Style in the Works of Paule Marshall." NALF, 9 (Fall 1975), 67, 71-76.

> Personal, political, and social growth of women protagonists in Marshall's three major works.

981     Marshall, Paule. "Shaping the World of My Art." NewL, 40 (Autumn 1973), 97-112.

> Early influences, major themes, and role of black literature.

982     _____. "Reading." MADEMOISELLE, 79 (June 1974), 82-83.

> Ralph Ellison's SHADOW AND ACT is an important influence on her work.

983     Nazareth, Peter. "Paule Marshall's Timeless People." NewL, 40 (Autumn 1973), 113-31.

> Roots, alienation, and exploitation of Third World people.

984     "The Negro Woman in American Literature." In KEEPING THE FAITH:

WRITINGS BY CONTEMPORARY BLACK WOMEN. Ed. Pat Crutchfield Exum. Greenwich, Conn.: Fawcett, 1974. Pp. 19-40.

Panel discussion on "The Negro Writer's Vision of America" at the New School for Social Research, New York, 1965. Participants include Sarah E. Wright, Abbey Lincoln, Alice Childress, and Paule Marshall.

985   Stoelting, Winifred L. "Time Past and Time Present: The Search for Viable Links in THE CHOSEN PLACE, THE TIMELESS PEOPLE by Paule Marshall." CLAJ, 16 (1972), 60-71.

Survival depends upon knowledge of a brutal past.


# JOHN A. WILLIAMS (1925- )

## Critical Studies

986   Browne, W. Francis. "The Black Artist in New York: An Interview with John A. Williams." CENTERPOINT, 1, No. 3 (1975), 71-76.

987   Bryant, Jerry H. "John A. Williams: The Political Use of the Novel." Crit, 16, iii (1975), 81-100.

Williams' subject is black struggle for manhood. His novels parellel themes of Wright and Baldwin.

988   Burke, William M. "The Resistance of John A. Williams: THE MAN WHO CRIED I AM." Crit, 15, iii (1973), 5-14.

MAN mixes fact and fiction.

989   Cash, Earl A. JOHN WILLIAMS: THE EVOLUTION OF A BLACK WRITER. New York: Third Press, 1975.

990   Fleming, Robert E. "The Nightmare Level of THE MAN WHO CRIED I AM." ConL, 14 (1973), 186-96.

Artistic possibilities in a grotesque underworld.

991   Gayle, Addison, Jr. THE WAY OF THE NEW WORLD: THE BLACK NOVEL IN AMERICA. Garden City, N.Y.: Anchor Press, Doubleday, 1975. Pp. 277-86.

Williams' novels progress "from protest to assertion, from a feeble optimism to a hard-learned reality." His strength lies in "the synthesis of fiction and history."

992   Georgakas, Dan. "John Williams at 49: An Interview." MinnR, 7 (1976), 51–65.

993   Kent, George E. "Outstanding Works in Black Literature During 1972." PHYLON, 34 (1973), 307–29.

CAPTAIN BLACKMAN is an inventive historical novel, but there is not much development in Blackman's character.

994   Klotman, Phyllis R. "An Examination of the Black Confidence Man in Two Black Novels: THE MAN WHO CRIED I AM and DEM." AL, 44 (1973), 596–611.

Williams' con man symbol of corruption vs Kelley's con man derived from folklore and Ralph Ellison's Rinehart.

995   O'Brien, John. "The Art of John A. Williams." (Interview). ASch, 42 (Summer 1973), 489–94, 96, 98; rpt. in INTERVIEWS WITH BLACK WRITERS. Ed. John O'Brien. New York: Liveright, 1973. Pp. 225–43.

996   Skerrett, Joseph T., Jr. "Novelist in Motion: An Interview with John A. Williams." BlackW, 25 (January 1976), 58–67, 93–97.

997   Walcott, Ronald. "The Early Fiction of John A. Williams." CLAJ, 16 (1972), 198–213.

Autobiographical roots of the major works. Also deals with the evolution of Williams' fictive world.

998   Williams, John A. "Black Publisher, Black Writer: An Impasse." BlackW, 26 (March 1975), 28–31.

See also Dudley, Randall. "Black Publisher, Black Writer: An Answer," BlackW, 26 (March 1975), 32–37.

999   _____. "The Crisis in American Letters." THE BLACK SCHOLAR, 6 (June 1975), 67–72.

Comments on black writers and their works.


## WILLIAM MELVIN KELLEY (1937-  )

## Bibliographies

See 1001, below.

## Critical Studies

1000   Baker, Houston A., Jr.   "A View of William Melvin Kelley's DEM."
OBSIDIAN, 3 (Summer 1977), 12-16.

> The white protagonist, an archetype, "vibrant in the undercon-
> sciousness of Black America," is portrayed with "scathing" and
> "liberating" humor reminiscent of folk animal tales and
> Baldwin's darkest rage.

1001   Beards, Richard.   "Parody as Tribute:  William Melvin Kelley's A DIF-
FERENT DRUMMER and Faulkner."   SBL, 5 (Winter 1974), 25-28.

> Kelley's use of Faulknerian techniques.   Article includes a
> Kelley checklist of primary and secondary sources, (p. 28).

1002   Eckley, Grace.   "The Awakening of Mr. Afrinnegan:  Kelley's DUN-
FORDS TRAVELS EVERYWHERES and Joyce's FINNEGANS WAKE."
OBSIDIAN, 1 (Summer 1975), 27-41.

> Joycean parallels in characters, setting, language, and use of
> mythology, especially the Scandinavian.

1003   Faulkner, Howard.   "The Uses of Tradition:  William Melvin Kelley's
A DIFFERENT DRUMMER."   MFS, 21 (1975), 535-42.

> Kelley uses the Bible, mythology, the tall-tale tradition,
> and the themes and techniques of William Faulkner.

1004   Gayle, Addison, Jr.   THE WAY OF THE NEW WORLD:  THE BLACK
NOVEL IN AMERICA.   Garden City, N.Y.:   Anchor Press, Doubleday,
1975.   Pp. 139-50.

> A DIFFERENT DRUMMER and DUNFORDS TRAVELS EVERY-
> WHERES deal with the continuing history, culture, and sepa-
> rate African identity of blacks despite the "Western night-
> mare."

1005   Ingrasci, Hugh J.   "Strategic Withdrawal or Retreat:  Deliverance from
Racial Oppression in Kelley's A DIFFERENT DRUMMER and Faulkner's
GO DOWN, MOSES."   SBL, 6 (Fall 1975), 1-6.

> A comparative study of Kelley's Tucker Caliban and Faulkner's
> Sam Fathers:  their struggle to liberate themselves from the
> racism of the South" (OBSIDIAN, see entry 1082).

1006   Klotman, Phyllis R.   "The Passive Resistant in A DIFFERENT DRUMMER,
DAY OF ABSENCE and MANY THOUSAND GONE."   SBL, 3 (Autumn
1972), 7-12.

> Running man as recurrent theme, his evasive action seen as
> a social not solitary act.

1007 _____. "An Examination of the Black Confidence Man in Two Black
Novels: THE MAN WHO CRIED I AM and DEM." AL, 44 (1973), 596-611.

For annotation see entry 994.

1008 Nadeau, Robert L. "Black Jesus: A Study of Kelley's A DIFFERENT
DRUMMER." SBL, 11 (Summer 1971), 13-15.

Kelley's attack on black stereotypes is comparable to trans-
cendentalist self-reliance.

1009 Rosenblatt, Roger. BLACK FICTION. Cambridge, Mass.: Harvard
Univ. Press, 1974. Pp. 142-50.

"DEM is about both ends of slavery, the black and white
products founded in part on a slave economy."

1010 Schatt, Stanley. "You Must Go Home Again: Today's Afro-American
Expatriate Writers." NALF, 7 (1973), 80-82.

A discussion of the recent fiction of William Gardner Smith
and William Melvin Kelley.

1011 Weyant, Jill. "The Kelley Saga: Violence in America." CLAJ, 19
(1975), 210-20.

Kelley's novels are related by theme and character to form a
kind of saga.

1012 Weyl, Donald M. "The Vision of Man in the Novels of William
Melvin Kelley." Crit, 15, iii (1973), 15-33.

Kelley exhibits an artistic decline from his earliest works because he moves away from real people to abstract characteri-
zations.

1013 Williams, Gladys M. "Technique as Evaluation of Subject in A DIF-
FERENT DRUMMER." CLAJ, 19 (1975), 221-37.

The technique integrates romance-myth, realism, and naturalism
to explore contradictions in American culture. Modes of narration vary according to which narrator tells the story.

See also 1119.

## ERNEST J. GAINES (1933- )

## Critical Studies

1014 Bryant, Jerry H. "From Death to Life: The Fiction of Ernest J.

Gaines." IowaR, 3 (Winter 1972), 106-20.

Gaines's fiction shows a movement toward a reconciliation of past and future: "Out of death grows life."

1015 _____. "Ernest J. Gaines: Change, Growth and History." SoR, 10 (1974), 851-64.

Earlier works lead to THE AUTOBIOGRAPHY OF MISS JANE PITTMAN, which combines "the human and political implications of his subject."

1016 Burke, William. "BLOODLINE: A Black Man's South." CLAJ, 19 (1976), 545-58.

Discusses the five stories in BLOODLINE whose "excellence" is demonstrated in two ways: "human" and "symbolic."

1017 Carter, Tom. "Ernest Gaines." ESSENCE, 6 (July 1975), 52-53, 71-72.

Zora Neale Hurston and his aunt Augusta influenced him.

1018 "Ernest J. Gaines." In INTERVIEWS WITH BLACK WRITERS. Ed. John O'Brien. New York: Liveright, 1973. Pp. 79-93.

1019 Gayle, Addison, Jr. THE WAY OF THE NEW WORLD: THE BLACK NOVEL IN AMERICA. Garden City, N.Y.: Anchor Press, Doubleday, 1975. Pp. 287-301.

How Gaines deals with the racial past.

1020 Laney, Ruth. "A Conversation with Ernest Gaines." SoR, 10 (1974), 1-14.

1021 McDonald, Walter R. "'You Not a Bum, You a Man': Ernest J. Gaines's BLOODLINE." NALF, 9 (Summer 1975), 47-49.

It is like an episodic novel unified by theme and setting.

1022 Schraufnagel, Noel. FROM APOLOGY TO PROTEST: THE BLACK AMERICAN NOVEL. Deland, Fla.: Everett, Edwards, 1973. Pp. 158-64.

CATHERINE CARMIER and OF LOVE AND DUST "stress the point that racism stems largely from sexual fears."

1023 Shelton, Frank W. "Ambiguous Manhood in Ernest J. Gaines's BLOOD-LINE." CLAJ, 19 (1975), 200-209.

His themes deal with the search for black manhood.

1024    Stoelting, Winifred L.   "Human Dignity and Pride in the Novels of
        Ernest Gaines."  CLAJ, 14 (1971), 340-58.

        His characters' dignity is emphasized above the correctness
        of choices they make.

1025    Tooker, Dan.  FICTION:  INTERVIEWS WITH NORTHERN CALIFORNIA
        NOVELISTS.  New York:  Harcourt, Brace Jovanovich, 1976.

        Interview with Ernest Gaines.

1026    Williams, Sherley Anne.  GIVE BIRTH TO BRIGHTNESS:  A THEMATIC
        STUDY IN NEO-BLACK LITERATURE.  New York:  Dial Press, 1972.

        For annotation see entry 973.

        See also 1119.


## ISHMAEL REED (1938-  )

## Critical Studies

1027    Ambler, Madge.  "Ishmael Reed:  Whose Radio Broke Down?"  NALF,
        6 (Winter 1972), 125-31.

        YELLOW BACK RADIO satirizes American church, emasculat-
        ing black women, Communist Party, histories degrading blacks,
        and so on.

1028    Baker, Houston A., Jr.  Rev. of THE LAST DAYS OF LOUISIANA
        RED by Ishmael Reed.  BlackW, 24 (June 1975), 51-52, 89.

        Not as original as earlier books.

1029    Beauford, Fred.  "A Conversation with Ishmael Reed."  BLACK CREA-
        TION, 4 (1973), 12-15.

1030    Bryant, Jerry H.  "Who?  Jes Grew?  Like Topsy?  No, Not Like
        Topsy."  THE NATION, 25 September 1972, pp. 245-47.

        MUMBO JUMBO is rich in allusion and imagination.

1031    Edwards, Thomas R.  "News from Elsewhere."  NYRB, 5 October 1972,
        pp. 21-23.

        MUMBO JUMBO shows the mythic possibilities of popular
        culture.

1032    Fenderson, Lewis H.  "The New Breed of Black Writers and Their

Jaundiced View of Tradition." CLAJ, 15 (1971), 18-24.

> American absurdity is reflected in the mass media. Best
> weapon blacks have is satire.

1033   Ford, Nick Aaron. "A Note on Ishmael Reed: Revolutionary Novelist."
SNNTS, 3 (1971), 216-18.

> Reed, the most revolutionary of black novelists, assaults
> through satire.

1034   Friedman, Alan. Rev. of MUMBO JUMBO by Ishmael Reed. NYTBR,
6 August 1972, pp. 1, 22.

> Reed's satire and farce are a cross between fiction and witch-
> craft.

1035   "Ishmael Reed." FICTION INTERNATIONAL, Summer 1973; rpt. in
INTERVIEWS WITH BLACK WRITERS. Ed. John O'Brien. New York:
Liveright, 1973. Pp. 165-83.

1036   "Ishmael Reed on Ishmael Reed." BlackW, 23 (June 1974), 20-34.

1037   O'Brien, John. "Ishmael Reed." (Interview). In THE NEW FICTION:
INTERVIEWS WITH INNOVATIVE AMERICAN WRITERS. Ed. Joe David
Bellamy. Urbana: Univ. of Illinois Press, 1974. Pp. 130-41.

> This interview was "conducted in several parts between 1971 and
> and 1973."

1038   Schmitz, Neil. "Neo-HooDoo: Experimental Fiction of Ishmael Reed."
TCL, 20 (1974), 126-40.

> Reed uses "Neo-HooDoo" to escape traditional fictive modes.

See also 1164.


# TONI MORRISON (1931-  )

## Critical Studies

1039   Bischoff, Joan. "The Novels of Toni Morrison." SBL, 6 (Fall 1975),
21-23.

> Variations of a Jamesian theme: the sensitivity of black
> children in THE BLUEST EYE and SULA.

1040   Blackburn, Sara. Rev. of SULA by Toni Morrison. NYTBR, 30 December 1973, p. 3.

Although "setting and the characters continually convince and intrigue, the novel seems somehow frozen, stylized."

1041  "Conversations with Alice Childress and Toni Morrison/The Co-Editors." BLACK CREATION ANNUAL, 6 (1974-75), pp. 90-92.

1042  Grant, Liz.  Rev. of THE BLUEST EYE by Toni Morrison.  BlackW, 20 (May 1971), 51-52.

Her theme of self-hatred has not been treated so well since Ralph Ellison's INVISIBLE MAN.

1043  Jefferson, Margo.  "Toni Morrison: Passionate and Precise."  MS., 3 December 1974, pp. 34-38.

SULA and THE BLUEST EYE are "passionate and precise . . . lyrical and philosophical."

1044  Kaiser, Ernest.  Rev. of SONG OF SOLOMON by Toni Morrison. FREEDOMWAYS, 17 (1977), 187.

All her characters are stereotypes.  Only whites like her.

1045  McClain, Ruth Rambo.  Rev. of SULA by Toni Morrison.  BlackW, 23 (June 1974), 51-53.

"Thought-provoking story . . . sophisticated symbols."

1046  Price, Reynolds.  Rev. of SONG OF SOLOMON by Toni Morrison. NYTBR, 11 September 1977, pp. 1, 48.

A masterpiece that surveys nearly a century of American history.  Not realism but fantasy, fable, song, and allegory.

1047  Sissman, L.E.  Rev. of THE BLUEST EYE by Toni Morrison.  THE NEW YORKER, 23 January 1971, pp. 92-94.

"Painful and acute" study of black childhood.

1048  Smith, Barbara.  Rev. of SULA by Toni Morrison.  FREEDOMWAYS, 14 (1974), 69-72.

Morrison is a "virtuoso" rooted in black life.  SULA is "beautiful, mysterious and needed."

1049  Watkins, Mel.  "Talk with Toni Morrison."  NYTBR, 11 September 1977, pp. 48, 50.

# Chapter 4
# BIBLIOGRAPHIES AND GENERAL STUDIES


## A. BIBLIOGRAPHIES

1050 AMERICAN LITERARY SCHOLARSHIP: AN ANNUAL. Ed. James
Woodress. Durham, N.C.: Duke Univ. Press, 1965-- .

An evaluation of what the ALS considers the most significant
criticisms of the year. The 1975 issue appeared in 1977, rep-
resenting as in the MLA INTERNATIONAL BIBLIOGRAPHY
(entry 1079) a two-year lapse. From 1969-74, ed. J.A.
Robbins.


1051 ANNUAL BIBLIOGRAPHY OF ENGLISH LANGUAGE AND LITERATURE.
Leeds, Engl.: Modern Humanities Research Association, 1920-- .

Comparable to bibliographies in MLA INTERNATIONAL BIBLI-
OGRAPHY (entry 1079). Lists essays of literary criticism and
scholarship in American and English journals. Three-year
lapse between initial publication of essays and their inclusion in the bibliography.


1052 Babour, James, and Robert E. Fleming. "A Checklist of Criticism on
Early Afro-American Novelists." CLAJ, 8 (1977), 21-26.

Lists general criticism as well as individual studies of William
Wells Brown, Charles Waddell Chesnutt, Martin R. Delany,
Paul Laurence Dunbar, Sutton E. Griggs, and Frank J. Webb.

1053 BIBLIOGRAPHICAL SURVEY: THE NEGRO IN PRINT. 3 vols. Washington, D.C.: The Negro Bibliographic and Research Center, 1965-1968.

Surveys published works in all fields.

1054 Bone, Robert A. "Bibliography." In his THE NEGRO NOVEL IN
AMERICA. Rev. ed. New Haven, Conn.: Yale Univ. Press, 1965.
Pp. 255-70.

This excellent bibliography contains "Full-length Novels Written by American Negroes, 1853-1952," "Novelettes, 1853-1952," "Periodical Literature, 1853-1952," and "Bibliographies and Autobiographies."

1055 _____. "Bibliography." In his DOWN HOME: A HISTORY OF AFRO-AMERICAN SHORT FICTION FROM ITS BEGINNINGS TO THE END OF THE HARLEM RENAISSANCE. New York: G.P. Putnam's Sons, 1975. Pp. 307-14.

Bibliography contains short story collections and uncollected stories by individual authors.

1056 Chapman, Abraham. THE NEGRO IN AMERICAN LITERATURE AND A BIBLIOGRAPHY OF AMERICAN LITERATURE BY AND ABOUT NEGRO AMERICANS. Stevens Point: Wisconsin State Univ., 1966.

A major source superseded by Corrigan; see entries 1059-61.

1057 CLA JOURNAL. "An Annual Bibliography of Afro-American Literature, 1975, With Selected Bibliographies of African and Caribbean Literature." Comp. Virginia Barrett et al. Vol. 20 (1976), 94-131.

Fairly thorough coverage.

1058 _____. "An Annual Bibliography of Afro-American, African and Caribbean Literature for the Year, 1976." Comp. Vattel T. Rose et al. Vol. 21 (1977), 100-157.

1059 Corrigan, Robert A. "Afro-American Fiction: A Checklist 1853-1970." MASJ, 11 (1970), 114-35.

A good comprehensive survey. A preliminary version was published in SBL, 1 (Summer 1970), 51-86.

1060 _____. "Afro-American Fiction: Errata and Additions." AmerS, 12 (Spring 1971), 69-73.

1061 _____. "Afro-American Fiction Since 1970." AmerS, 14 (Fall 1973), 85-90.

An update of the above.

1062 _____, comp. RICHARD WRIGHT AND HIS INFLUENCE. Iowa City: Univ. of Iowa, 1971.

First of two volumes prepared and distributed in a limited number of copies to conferees of the Third Annual Institute for Afro-American Culture, July 1971. Chapters in this volume concerning Afro-American fiction are the following: "Richard Wright Criticism: A Preliminary Checklist"; Robert A. Corrigan, "Bibliography of Afro-American Fiction: 1853-1971"; Lynn Munro, "Periodicalized and Anthologized Afro-American Short Fiction: A Preliminary Bibliography." See also entries 873-74.

1063 Deodene, Frank, and William P. French. BLACK AMERICAN FICTION SINCE 1952; A PRELIMINARY CHECKLIST. Chatham, N.J.: Chatham Bookseller, 1970.

An accurate listing with brief plot annotations. Supplements Whiteman, entry 1094, to mid-1969.

1064 DuBois, W.E. Burghardt, ed. A SELECT BIBLIOGRAPHY OF THE NEGRO AMERICAN. Atlanta, Ga.: Atlanta Univ. Press, 1905.

One of the earliest bibliographies, but covers all fields.

1065 FREEDOMWAYS. "Recent Books." Comp. Ernest Kaiser. 1961-- .

Almost from its inception in 1961 this quarterly has included a useful annotated listing of new books on black subjects.

1066 Gloster, Hugh. "Bibliography." In his NEGRO VOICES IN AMERICAN FICTION. Chapel Hill: Univ. of North Carolina Press, 1948; rpt. New York: Russell & Russell, 1965. Pp. 273-88.

Bibliography contains "Fiction by Negro Authors," "Literary History and Criticism," "Magazine Articles and Reviews," "Newspaper Articles and Reviews," "Anthologies," and "Background Material."

1067 GUIDE TO REPRINTS 1967-- . Annual.

A cumulative guide to books, journals, and other materials which are available in reprint form.

1068 Homer, Dorothy R., and Ann H. Swartout. BOOKS ABOUT THE NEGRO: AN ANNOTATED BIBLIOGRAPHY. New York: Praeger, 1966.

1069 Houston, Helen Ruth. THE AFRO-AMERICAN NOVEL, 1965-1975: A DESCRIPTIVE BIBLIOGRAPHY OF PRIMARY AND SECONDARY MATERIAL. Troy, N.Y.: Whitston Publishing Co., 1977.

Especially helpful with newer authors.

1070 Howard University Library, Washington, D.C. DICTIONARY CATALOG

OF THE JESSE E. MOORLAND COLLECTION OF NEGRO LIFE AND HISTORY. 9 vols. Boston: G.K. Hall, 1970; 1st supp., 3 vols., 1976.

1071   Inge, M. Thomas, Jackson R. Bryer, and Maurice Duke, eds. BLACK AMERICAN WRITERS: BIBLIOGRAPHIC ESSAYS. 2 vols. New York: St. Martin's Press, 1978.

Volume 1: "The Beginnings through the Harlem Renaissance and Langston Hughes," by Blyden Jackson, et al. Volume 2: "Richard Wright, Ralph Ellison, James Baldwin, and Imamu Amiri Baraka," by John M. Reilly, et al. Contains essays on many fiction writers, with an extensive and detailed evaluation of secondary sources.

1072   Kirby, David K., ed. AMERICAN FICTION TO 1900: A GUIDE TO INFORMATION SOURCES. Detroit: Gale Research Co., 1975.

1073   Loggins, Vernon. "Bibliographies." In his THE NEGRO AUTHOR: HIS DEVELOPMENT IN AMERICA TO 1900. New York: Columbia Univ. Press, 1931. Rpt. Port Washington, N.Y.: Kennikat Press, 1964. Pp. 408-57.

Contains good nineteenth-century bibliography of fiction and other works.

1074   McDowell, Robert E., and George Fortenberry. "A Checklist of Books and Essays About American Negro Novelists." SNNTS, 3 (1971), 219-36.

This bibliography of secondary sources, both general and on individual authors, is extensive for Wright, Ellison, and Baldwin, but too brief for all other authors.

1075   McPherson, James M., et al. BLACKS IN AMERICA: BIBLIOGRAPHICAL ESSAYS. Garden City, N.Y.: Doubleday, 1971.

Contains a brief essay on fiction.

1076   Matthews, Geraldine O., and the African-American Materials Project Staff, comps. BLACK AMERICAN WRITERS, 1773-1949: A BIBLIOGRAPHY AND UNION LIST. Boston: G.K. Hall, 1975.

Listings of writers in all fields.

1077   Miller, Elizabeth W. THE NEGRO IN AMERICA: A BIBLIOGRAPHY. 2nd ed., rev. Cambridge, Mass.: Harvard Univ. Press, 1970.

Brief listing of some works of fiction.

1078   MLA ABSTRACTS. New York: Modern Language Association, 1970-1975.

The first issue annotating articles published in 1970 appeared in 1972. An annual, it was discontinued after 1975 volume, published 1977.

1079   MLA INTERNATIONAL BIBLIOGRAPHY. New York: Modern Language Association, 1921-- . Annual.

Listings of secondary sources. A two-year lapse between the listings and initial publications.

1080   Myers, Carol. "A Selected Bibliography of Recent Afro-American Writers." CLAJ, 16 (1973), 377-82.

Works not included in Darwin Turner. See entry 1092.

1081   New York Public Library. SCHOMBURG COLLECTION OF NEGRO LITERATURE AND HISTORY. DICTIONARY CATALOG. 9 vols. Boston: G.K. Hall, 1962; 1st supplement 1968, 2 vols.; 2d supplement 1972, 4 vols.

Lists manuscripts, correspondence, microfilms, and related materials of major Afro-American writers, as well as a compendious collection of the works of all Afro-American authors. As of 1975 the BIBLIOGRAPHIC GUIDE TO BLACK STUDIES (G.K. Hall) serves as an annual supplement to the DICTIONARY CATALOG.

1082   OBSIDIAN. "Studies in Afro-American Literature: An Annual Annotated Bibliography." Ed. and comp. Charles H. Rowell. 1975-- . 3/year.

This new periodical of black literature in review promises to carry an annual annotated bibliography. With only a one-year lapse between initial publication of essays and their inclusion here, the first two years' bibliographies are well done.

1083   Olsson, Martin. A SELECTED BIBLIOGRAPHY OF BLACK LITERATURE: THE HARLEM RENAISSANCE. Exeter, Engl.: University of Exeter, 1973.

This is a sketchy resource.

1084   Page, James A., comp. SELECTED BLACK AMERICAN AUTHORS: AN ILLUSTRATED BIO-BIBLIOGRAPHY. Boston: G.K. Hall, 1977.

Thumbnail sketches of authors accompanied for the most part by photographs. Some errors.

1085    PHYLON.  Variously titled, annual survey of Afro-American literature.
        1940--.

        PHYLON is useful but not as extensive as surveys in other
        periodicals cited above.

1086    Porter, Dorothy B.  THE NEGRO IN THE UNITED STATES: A SELECTED
        BIBLIOGRAPHY.  Washington, D.C.:  Library of Congress, 1970.

        Porter cumulates her earlier, preliminary bibliographies pub-
        lished in 1945 and 1969.

1087    Robbins, J. Albert, et al., eds.  AMERICAN LITERARY MANUSCRIPTS:
        A CHECKLIST OF HOLDINGS IN ACADEMIC, HISTORICAL, AND
        PUBLIC LIBRARIES, MUSEUMS, AND AUTHORS' HOMES IN THE
        UNITED STATES.  2nd ed.  Athens, Ga.:  Univ. of Georgia Press,
        1977.

        Compiled by mailed questionnaires.  Fragmentary.

1088    Rowell, Charles H.  "A Bibliography of Bibliographies for the Study of
        Black American Literature and Folklore."  BLACK EXPERIENCE, A
        SOUTHERN UNIVERSITY JOURNAL, 55 (June 1969), 95-111.

1089    Rush, Theressa Gunnels, Carol Fairbanks Myers, and Esther Spring
        Arata.  BLACK AMERICAN WRITERS PAST AND PRESENT: A BIO-
        GRAPHICAL AND BIBLIOGRAPHICAL DICTIONARY.  2 vols.  Metu-
        chen, N.J.:  Scarecrow Press, 1975.

        Despite some ambiguity about genre and errors in dates, this is
        a very helpful compendium, especially for lesser-known writers.

1090    Schatz, Walter, ed.  DIRECTORY OF AFRO-AMERICAN RESOURCES.
        New York:  R.R. Bowker, 1970.

        Compiled this by mailed questionnaires, telephone inquiries,
        and personal visits.  Fragmentary and inconsistent.

1091    Shockley, Ann Allen, and Sue P. Chandler.  LIVING BLACK AMERI-
        CAN AUTHORS: A BIOGRAPHICAL DIRECTORY.  New York:  R.R.
        Bowker, 1973.

        Does not include a number of authors.

1092    Turner, Darwin T.  AFRO-AMERICAN WRITERS.  New York:  Appleton-
        Century-Crofts, 1970.

        Good, but not all inclusive.  See Myers, above, for works
        not in Turner.

1093   Van Deusen, John G. "Bibliography." In his THE BLACK MAN IN WHITE AMERICA. Rev. ed. Washington, D.C.: Associated Publishers, 1944. Pp. 335-53.

General bibliography of "Books and Pamphlets" which contains some works of Afro-American fiction.

1094   Whiteman, Maxwell. A CENTURY OF FICTION BY AMERICAN NEGROES, 1853-1952. Philadelphia: Press of Maurice Jacobs, 1955; rpt. Philadelphia: Albert Saifer, 1974.

A standard bibliography with brief annotation of plots. See entry 1063 for supplement to mid-1969.

1095   Whitlow, Roger. "Black American Literature: A Bibliography of Folklore, Poetry, Autobiography, Fiction, Drama, Anthologies, Literary Criticism and Bibliography, and Social and Historical Comment." In his BLACK AMERICAN LITERATURE: A CRITICAL HISTORY. Chicago: Nelson-Hall, 1973. Pp. 197-271.

An extensive bibliography of primary and secondary sources, with a number of omissions.

1096   _____. "The Harlem Renaissance and After: A Checklist of Black Literature of the Twenties and Thirties." NALF, 7 (1973), 143-46.

1097   Williams, Ora. "A Bibliography of Works Written by American Black Women." CLAJ, 15 (1972), 354-77.

1098   _____. AMERICAN BLACK WOMEN IN THE ARTS AND SOCIAL SCIENCES: A BIBLIOGRAPHIC SURVEY. Metuchen, N.J.: Scarecrow Press, 1973; rev. ed., 1978.

1099   Woodress, James, ed. AMERICAN FICTION, 1900-1950: A GUIDE TO INFORMATION SOURCES. Detroit: Gale Research Co., 1974.

1100   Work, Monroe N., comp. A BIBLIOGRAPHY OF THE NEGRO IN AFRICA AND AMERICA. New York: H.W. Wilson, 1928; rpt. New York: Octagon Books, 1965.

Cites some obscure titles but does not always indicate genre.

## B. GENERAL STUDIES

This listing of the materials includes the most representative works dealing exclusively with Afro-American culture and fiction. Reprints are occasionally cited for titles of significant literary or historic importance.

1101 THE AMERICAN NEGRO WRITER AND HIS ROOTS. Selected Papers from the First Conference of Negro Writers, March 1959. New York: American Society of African Culture, 1960.

> Papers by Saunders Redding, Samuel W. Allen, John Henrik Clarke, Julian Mayfield, Arthur P. Davis, Langston Hughes, William Branch, Arna Bontemps, Loften Mitchell, Sara E. Wright, and John O. Killens.

1102 Baker, Houston A., Jr. SINGERS OF DAYBREAK: STUDIES IN BLACK AMERICAN LITERATURE. Washington, D.C.: Howard Univ. Press, 1974.

> Essays on Wright, Ellison, Toomer, George Cain, Dunbar, James Weldon Johnson, Malcolm X, and Gwendolyn Brooks.

1103 Bell, Bernard W. "Literary Sources of the Early Afro-American Novel." CLAJ, 18 (1974), 29–43.

> Cites slave narratives, the Bible, and popular fiction as literary sources.

1104 Bigsby, C.W.E., ed. THE BLACK AMERICAN WRITER: VOLUME 1 -- FICTION. Deland, Fla.: Everett, Edwards, 1969.

> Contributions by C.W.E. Bigsby, Richard Gilman, Theodore Gross, Langston Hughes, John A. Williams, William Gardner Smith, Robert Farnsworth, Warren French, Ralph Ellison, James Baldwin, Wilson Record, Hoyt W. Fuller, and others.

1105 BLACK WORLD, 20 (November 1970).

> Special issue about Harlem Renaissance, containing articles on Claude McKay, Jean Toomer, Arna Bontemps, Jessie Fauset, Zora Neale Hurston, Wallace Thurman, and Rudolph Fisher.

1106 Bone, Robert A. THE NEGRO NOVEL IN AMERICA. Rev. ed. New Haven, Conn.: Yale Univ. Press, 1965.

> A comprehensive critical survey. The Negro novel alternates between assimilative and nationalistic tendencies.

1107 _____. DOWN HOME: A HISTORY OF AFRO-AMERICAN SHORT FICTION FROM ITS BEGINNINGS TO THE END OF THE HARLEM RENAISSANCE. New York: G.P. Putnam's Sons, 1975.

Short fiction from pastoral motifs to nonpastoral shifts and revolutionary.

1108  Brawley, Benjamin. THE NEGRO IN LITERATURE AND ART IN THE UNITED STATES. New York: Duffield, 1930; rpt. New York: AMS, 1971.

Intended for "classes and clubs," the book is outdated but has historical interest as a contemporary overview of Afro-American culture.

1109  Bronz, Stephen H. ROOTS OF NEGRO RACIAL CONSCIOUSNESS: THE 1920'S: THREE HARLEM RENAISSANCE WRITERS. New York: Libra Publishers, 1964.

Brief study of the poetry and fiction of James Weldon Johnson, Countee Cullen, and Claude McKay.

1110  Brown, Lloyd. "The West Indian as an Ethnic Stereotype in Black American Literature." NALF, 1 (Spring 1971), 8-14.

The "stereotype of the monkey-chaser is giving way to an archetype of revolutionary black consciousness."

1111  _____. THE BLACK WRITER IN AFRICA AND THE AMERICAS. Los Angeles: Hennessey & Ingalls, 1973.

Articles on Afro-American literature by Abraham Chapman, Nick Aaron Ford, John F. Bayliss, James A. Emanuel, Edward Margolies, and Mercer A. Cook.

1112  Brown, Sterling A. NEGRO POETRY AND DRAMA, AND THE NEGRO IN AMERICAN FICTION. Washington, D.C.: Associates in Negro Folk Education, 1937; rpt. New York: Atheneum, 1969.

This was originally published separately but reprinted as one volume. An undergraduate textbook but contains good information.

1113  _____. "The Negro Author and His Publisher." THE QUARTERLY REVIEW OF HIGHER EDUCATION AMONG NEGROES, 9 (1941), 140-46.

The Negro author must develop a "critical but interested public" in order to overcome publishers' prejudices and preconceptions.

1114  Brown, Sterling A., Arthur P. Davis, and Ulysses Lee, eds. THE NEGRO CARAVAN. New York: Dryden Press, 1941; rpt. New York: Arno Press, 1969.

A superb anthology containing excellent essays on fiction and other genres.

1115    Butcher, Margaret. THE NEGRO IN AMERICAN CULTURE. New York: Alfred A. Knopf, 1956.

Butcher based this work on a manuscript left by Alain Locke. Contains material on Afro-American writings.

1116    Calverton, V.F., ed. ANTHOLOGY OF NEGRO LITERATURE. New York: Random House, 1929.

Calverton is an important Marxist critic, and his book is a historically important pioneer anthology of Afro-American writing. It contains an introduction, "The Growth of Negro Literature," by Calverton, pp. 1-17.

1117    Chapman, Abraham. "The Harlem Renaissance in Literary History." CLAJ, 11 (1967), 38-58.

The historical, cultural, and literary significance of the New Negro movement has been unjustifiably neglected in most studies of American literary history.

1118    CLA JOURNAL, 17 (March 1974).

Special issue on Richard Wright, Ralph Ellison, and James Baldwin.

1119    _____, 19 (December 1975).

Special issue on "Afro-American Prose Fiction and Verse." Contains articles on Chesnutt, McKay, Ellison, Baldwin, Gaines, Kelley, and Alice Walker.

1120    Cooke, M.G., ed. MODERN BLACK NOVELISTS: A COLLECTION OF CRITICAL ESSAYS. Englewood Cliffs, N.J.: Prentice-Hall, 1971.

Included are previously published pieces on American, African, and West Indian authors. Has articles on Afro-American fiction by Robert Bone, Jonathan Baumbach, Kingsley Widmer, and Michel Fabre.

1121    Cruse, Harold. THE CRISIS OF THE NEGRO INTELLECTUAL. New York: William Morrow, 1967.

The development of a black capitalist class that gives independent support to black culture is a prerequisite to Negro political freedoms and equality. Much attention is given to the failures of the Harlem Renaissance in this regard.

1122    Davis, Arthur P. FROM THE DARK TOWER: AFRO-AMERICAN
WRITERS, 1900 TO 1960. Washington, D.C.: Howard Univ. Press,
1974.

Overview of significant writers and their works.

1123    Dickstein, Morris. "Black Writing and Black Nationalism: Four Generations." In his GATES OF EDEN: AMERICAN CULTURE IN THE
SIXTIES. New York: Basic Books, 1977. Pp. 154–82.

The 1960s successfully married literature to ideology in the
works of Eldridge Cleaver, George Cain, and Cecil Brown.
Dickstein traces this development from Richard Wright via
James Baldwin and Ralph Ellison.

1124    Ford, Nick Aaron. THE CONTEMPORARY NEGRO NOVEL: A STUDY
IN RACE RELATIONS. Boston: Meador Publishing Co., 1936.

Ford based this work on his M.A. thesis, University of Iowa,
presented in 1934 under title "A Study of the Race Problem
As It Appears in Contemporary Novels Written by Negroes."
Bibliography, pp. 107–8.

1125    Gayle, Addison, Jr. "The Harlem Renaissance: Towards a Black Aesthetic." MASJ, 11 (Fall 1970), 78–87.

Elements of race pride and unity in the 1920s suggest the
beginnings of a "black aesthetic."

1126    _____. THE WAY OF THE NEW WORLD: THE BLACK NOVEL IN
AMERICA. Garden City, N.Y.: Anchor Press, Doubleday, 1975.

An interesting critique from the point of view of the "black
aesthetic," but a number of important authors are neglected.

1127    _____, ed. BLACK EXPRESSION: ESSAYS BY AND ABOUT BLACK
AMERICANS IN THE CREATIVE ARTS. New York: Weybright and
Talley, 1969.

Five original essays and many reprints. One section of twenty
pieces on fiction, and a two-page list of suggested readings
about black fiction.

1128    _____. THE BLACK AESTHETIC. Garden City, N.Y.: Doubleday,
1971.

Writings by various authors on different aspects of the "Black
Aesthetic"; one section devoted to fiction contains essays by
Richard Wright, Hoyt W. Fuller, John Oliver Killens,
Ishmael Reed, and others.

1129    Gerard, Albert. LES TAMBOURS DU NEANT: ESSAI SUR LE PROB-
        LEME EXISTENTIEL DANS LE ROMAN AMERICAIN. Brussels: La
        Renaissance du Livre, 1969.

        Discusses existentialist elements in Wright, Ellison, and
        Baldwin, pp. 149-91.

1130    Gibson, Donald B., ed. FIVE BLACK WRITERS: ESSAYS ON WRIGHT,
        ELLISON, BALDWIN, HUGHES AND LEROI JONES. New York: New
        York Univ. Press, 1970.

        Twenty-six pieces, many of them reprints.

1131    Gilman, Richard. "White Standards and Black Writing" and "Black
        Writing and White Criticism." In his THE CONFUSION OF REALMS.
        New York: Random House, 1969. Pp. 3-12, 13-21.

        A white critic defends the black aesthetic. The black experi-
        ence is so different from white concepts of reality that whites
        are incapable of assessing the writings of Afro-Americans.

1132    Gloster, Hugh. NEGRO VOICES IN AMERICAN FICTION. Chapel
        Hill: Univ. of North Carolina Press, 1948; rpt. New York: Russell
        & Russell, 1965.

        A solid survey of Afro-American novels and short fiction, with
        excellent plot summaries.

1133    Gross, Seymour L., and John Edward Hardy, eds. IMAGES OF THE
        NEGRO IN AMERICAN LITERATURE. Chicago: Univ. of Chicago
        Press, 1966.

        Reprints pieces by Leslie A. Fiedler, Ralph Ellison, Arthur P.
        Davis, Irving Howe, James Baldwin, Marcus Klein, Robert A.
        Bone, and others, with a good introduction and bibliography
        by Seymour L. Gross.

1134    Gross, Theodore L. "The Black Hero." In his THE HEROIC IDEAL IN
        AMERICAN LITERATURE. New York: Free Press, 1971. Pp. 125-89.

        Brief interpretative remarks on black writers with emphasis on
        Wright, Baldwin, and Ellison are included. The black hero is
        basically idealistic in opposing white authority.

1135    Gysin, Fritz. THE GROTESQUE IN AMERICAN NEGRO FICTION.
        JEAN TOOMER, RICHARD WRIGHT AND RALPH ELLISON. Bern,
        Switzerland: Francke Verlag, 1975.

1136    Hemenway, Robert, ed. THE BLACK NOVELIST. Columbus, Ohio:
        Charles E. Merrill, 1970.

Articles on Sutton E. Griggs, Charles W. Chesnutt, Paul Laurence Dunbar, Jessie Fauset, Zora Neale Hurston, Frank Yerby, Richard Wright, Ralph Ellison, James Baldwin, Claude McKay, and Jean Toomer. Bibliography.

1137    Hill, Herbert, ed. ANGER, AND BEYOND: THE NEGRO WRITER IN THE UNITED STATES. New York: Harper & Row, 1966.

Essays on various aspects of black literature by Saunders Redding, Arna Bontemps, Horace R. Cayton, LeRoi Jones, Robert Bone, Albert Murray, and others.

1138    Himes, Chester. "Dilemma of the Negro Novelist in the United States." In BEYOND THE ANGRY BLACK. Ed. John A. Williams. New York: Cooper Square Publishers, 1966. Pp. 51-58.

The Negro novelist must overcome the resistance in himself about the bitterness of his own life and must struggle with his environment, publishers, and public (black and white) who do not want to know the truth.

1139    Huggins, Nathan I. HARLEM RENAISSANCE. New York: Oxford Univ. Press, 1971.

In the main a social and cultural history, but solid information about the writers of the period.

1140    Hughes, Carl Milton. THE NEGRO NOVELIST: A DISCUSSION OF THE WRITINGS OF AMERICAN NEGRO NOVELISTS, 1940-1950. New York: Citadel Press, 1953.

Hughes surveys major writers of the 1940s.

1141    Jackson, Blyden. "The Negro's Image of the Universe as Reflected in His Fiction." CLAJ, 4 (1960), 22-31; rpt. in his THE WAITING YEARS: ESSAYS ON AMERICAN NEGRO LITERATURE. Baton Rouge: Louisiana State Univ. Press, 1976. Pp. 92-102.

The look, feel, and essence of the universe of Negro writers is remarkably static and impoverished.

1142    _____. "The Negro's Negro in Negro Literature." MQR, 4 (1965), 290-95.

Negro literature is beginning to move away from depicting a single character type.

1143    _____. THE WAITING YEARS: ESSAYS ON AMERICAN NEGRO LITERATURE. Baton Rouge: Louisiana State Univ. Press, 1976.

1144    John, Janheinz.  NEO-AFRICAN LITERATURE:  A HISTORY OF BLACK
        WRITING.  New York:  Grove Press, 1969.

        A general survey of African, Caribbean, and Afro-American
        literature by a noted German scholar in the field.


1145    Johnson, James Weldon.  "The Dilemma of the Negro Author."  AMERI-
        CAN MERCURY, 15 (1928), 477-81.

        Negro writers face two different audiences, black and white,
        each of whom makes different demands about the kind of mate-
        rial he may write.  A combined black and white readership
        may come after the breakdown of traditional stereotypes.


1146    Klotman, Phyllis R.  ANOTHER MAN GONE:  THE BLACK RUNNER
        IN CONTEMPORARY AFRO-AMERICAN LITERATURE.  Port Washington,
        N.Y.:  Kennikat Press, 1976.

        Links the archetypal fugitive in Western literature to his
        counterparts in American letters and especially in Afro-
        American writings from slave narratives to John A. Williams.


1147    Littlejohn, David.  BLACK ON WHITE:  A CRITICAL SURVEY OF
        WRITING BY AMERICAN NEGROES.  New York:  Grossman, 1966.

        Not generally appreciative of black writing.  Sees works
        mainly as race war literature.


1148    Locke, Alain.  "The Negro's Contribution to American Art and Litera-
        ture."  ANNALS OF THE AMERICAN ACADEMY OF POLITICAL AND
        SOCIAL SCIENCE, 140 (1928), 234-37.

        The younger generation of Negro writers stands "artistically
        self-sufficient and innerly controlled" as opposed to an older
        generation of authors who deal with social problems.


1149    _____, ed.  THE NEW NEGRO:  AN INTERPRETATION.  New York:
        Albert & Charles Boni, 1925; rpt. New York:  Atheneum, 1968.

        This historic anthology deals with the intellectual, cultural,
        and artistic aims of the New Negro movement.  For fic-
        tion, see especially essays by Alain Locke and William
        Braithwaite.

1150    Logan, Rayford, ed.  THE NEW NEGRO THIRTY YEARS AFTERWARD.
        Washington, D.C.:  Howard Univ. Press, 1955.

        Various papers on Alain Locke and historical, sociological, and
        cultural settings of the New Negro movement of the twenties
        and its subsequent development.  See especially Sterling Brown's
        survey, "The New Negro in Literature (1925-1955)," pp. 57-72.

1151   Loggins, Vernon. THE NEGRO AUTHOR: HIS DEVELOPMENT IN
       AMERICA TO 1900. New York: Columbia Univ. Press, 1931; rpt.
       Port Washington, N.Y.: Kennikat Press, 1964.

       A solid pioneering survey.


1152   Margolies, Edward. NATIVE SONS: A CRITICAL STUDY OF
       TWENTIETH-CENTURY NEGRO AMERICAN AUTHORS. Philadelphia
       and New York: J.B. Lippincott, 1968.

       Critical essays on Attaway, Baldwin, Wright, Himes, Ellison,
       Demby, and others.


1153   _____. "The Image of the Primitive in Black Letters." MASJ, 11
       (Fall 1970), 67-77.

       The image of the primitive persists in varied form from turn-
       of-the-century to Chester Himes.


1154   Meier, August. "Some Reflections on the Negro Novel." CLAJ, 2
       (1959), 168-77.

       An extremely favorable assessment of Robert Bone's THE NE-
       GRO NOVEL IN AMERICA. See also entry 1165.


1155   Muraskin, William. "An Alienated Elite: Short Stories in THE CRISIS,
       1910-1950." JOURNAL OF BLACK STUDIES, 1 (1971), 282-305.

       THE CRISIS stories from 1910-50 by alienated Negro middle-
       class authors demonstrate perceptions different from those of
       poor blacks.


1156   O'Brien, John, ed. INTERVIEWS WITH BLACK WRITERS. New York:
       Liveright, 1973.

       Thirteen original and four reprinted interviews with Arna
       Bontemps, Cyrus Colter, William Demby, Owen Dodson,
       Ralph Ellison, Ernest J. Gaines, Michael Harper, Robert
       Hayden, Clarence Major, Julian Mayfield, Ann Petry,
       Ishmael Reed, Alice Walker, John Wideman, John A.
       Williams, Charles Wright, and Al Young.


1157   Peden, William. "The Black Explosion." SSF, 7 (1975), 231-41.

       Surveys stories by Hughes, Wright, Himes, Baldwin, Petry,
       Cyrus Colter, Alice Walker, Ernest Gaines, Ed Bullins, and
       James Alan McPherson.


1158   Perry, Margaret. SILENCE TO THE DRUMS: A SURVEY OF THE
       LITERATURE OF THE HARLEM RENAISSANCE. Westport, Conn.:
       Greenwood Press, 1976.

Scrutinizes Harlem Renaissance writers, and their social and environmental backgrounds, and also deals with the high point and waning of the movement.

1159    Redding, Saunders. "The Problems of the Negro Writer." MR, 6 (1964–65), 57–70.

Too many Negro writers "deplore the fact that their identity as Negroes precludes their identification with American writing." Authors like Wright, Petry, Mayfield, and Ellison have transcended "assumptions" about Negroes; and theirs is both an American and Negro literature.

1160    Rosenblatt, Roger. BLACK FICTION. Cambridge, Mass.: Harvard Univ. Press, 1974.

Some rather dubious generalizations about the cyclic nature of Afro-American letters. Many important writers and their works are simply overlooked.

1161    Schraufnagel, Noel. FROM APOLOGY TO PROTEST: THE BLACK AMERICAN NOVEL. Deland, Fla.: Everett, Edwards, 1973.

Surveys major novels, 1940–70.

1162    Seyersted, Per. "A Survey of Trends and Figures in Afro-American Fiction." AMERICAN STUDIES IN SCANDINAVIA, 6 (1974), 67–86.

Emphasis on post-Wright fiction, noting trends toward nationalism and thence to common humanity.

1163    Singh, Amritjit. THE NOVELS OF THE HARLEM RENAISSANCE. University Park and London: Pennsylvania State Univ. Press, 1976.

Good critical survey of twelve writers, with some errors in the otherwise comprehensive bibliography.

1164    STUDIES IN THE NOVEL, 3 (Summer 1971).

Special issue on American Negro novelists, containing articles on James Baldwin, Richard Wright, Jean Toomer, and Ishmael Reed. Includes a checklist of books and essays about many important writers. See also McDowell and Fortenberry, above (1074).

1165    Turner, Darwin T. "THE NEGRO NOVEL IN AMERICA: In Rebuttal." CLAJ, 10 (1966), 122–34.

"Though often critically perceptive Robert Bone's NEGRO NOVEL is badly marred by his predilection to play the role of psychiatrist, philosopher and teacher for all Negroes." See also 1154.

1166 _____. IN A MINOR CHORD: THREE AFRO-AMERICAN WRITERS AND THEIR SEARCH FOR IDENTITY. Carbondale: Southern Illinois Press, 1971.

> Deals with Jean Toomer, Countee Cullen, and Zora Neale Hurston. Selected bibliography of primary and secondary sources.

1167 Turpin, Walters E. "Four Short Fiction Writers of the Harlem Renaissance--Their Legacy of Achievement." CLAJ, 11 (1967), 59-72.

> Analyses of Toomer's "Blood-Burning Moon" and stories by Jean Toomer, Rudolph Fisher, Langston Hughes, and Claude McKay that serve as models for later writers.

1168 Van Deusen, John G. "The Negro's Contribution to American Literature." In his THE BLACK MAN IN WHITE AMERICA. Washington, D.C.: Associated Publishers, 1938; rev. ed. 1944, pp. 265-86.

> Good general survey of black letters from Phillis Wheatley to Richard Wright.

1169 Waniek, Marilyn Nelson. "The Space Where Sex Should Be: Toward a Definition of the Black Literary Tradition." SBL, 6 (Fall 1975), 7-13.

> Examines Johnson's AUTOBIOGRAPHY OF AN EX-COLORED MAN, Ellison's INVISIBLE MAN, and Wright's NATIVE SON to show that there is so little sex in black American literature because black characters are too busy with racial confrontations.

1170 White, Walter. "Negro Literature." In AMERICAN WRITERS ON AMERICAN LITERATURE: BY THIRTY-SEVEN CONTEMPORARY WRITERS. Ed. John A. Macy. New York: Horace Liveright, 1931; rpt. Westport, Conn.: Greenwood Press, 1977. Pp. 442-51.

> The Harlem Renaissance broke minstrel stereotypes.

1171 Whitlow, Roger. BLACK AMERICAN LITERATURE: A CRITICAL HISTORY. Chicago: Nelson-Hall, 1973.

> A brief survey from origins to John A. Williams, dealing with folklore as well as poetry and fiction. Contains an extensive bibliography of primary and secondary sources.

1172 Williams, Sherley Anne. GIVE BIRTH TO BRIGHTNESS: A THEMATIC STUDY IN NEO-BLACK LITERATURE. New York: Dial Press, 1972.

> For annotation, see entry 973.

# Bibliographies and General Studies

1173  Young, James O.  BLACK WRITERS OF THE THIRTIES.  Baton Rouge:
      Louisiana State Univ. Press, 1973.

> Examines the decade, but does not include all writers.  A
> major theme relates how depression years changed the outlook
> of younger black authors.

# APPENDIX

A Chronological Bibliography of Afro-American Fiction, 1853-1976. Asterisks (*) indicate collections of short fiction by individual authors. The number after title in the entries below refers to the main entry in this guide where complete publication information is given.

1853    William Wells Brown. CLOTEL; OR, THE PRESIDENT'S DAUGHTER: A NARRATIVE OF SLAVE LIFE IN THE UNITED STATES. 65.

1857    Frank J. Webb. THE GARIES AND THEIR FRIENDS. 644.

1859    Martin R. Delany. BLAKE, OR THE HUTS OF AMERICA. 121.

1867    Lorenzo D. Blackson. THE RISE AND PROGRESS OF THE KINGDOMS OF LIGHT AND DARKNESS. 36.

1871    Thomas Detter. NELLIE BROWN, OR THE JEALOUS WIFE. 138.

1881    *T.T. Purvis. HAGAR, THE SINGING MAIDEN, WITH OTHER STORIES AND RHYMES. 801.

1886    James H.W. Howard. BOND AND FREE; A TRUE TALE OF SLAVE TIMES. 299.

1887    R.C.O. Benjamin. THE DEFENDER OF OBADIAH CUFF. 29.

1892    Frances Ellen Watkins Harper. IOLA LEROY; OR, SHADOWS UPLIFTED. 254.

        Emma Dunham Kelley [pseud. Forget-Me-Not]. MEGDA. 355.

1893    Victoria Earle (Victoria Earle Matthews). AUNT LINDY, A STORY FOUNDED ON REAL LIFE. 162.

# Appendix

1894    Amelia E. Johnson. THE HAZELEY FAMILY. 328.

Walter H. Stowers and William H. Anderson [pseud. Sanda]. AP-POINTED. 586.

1895    *M.L. Burgess. AVE MARIA. 739.

*Alice Ruth Moore (Nelson) Dunbar. VIOLETS AND OTHER TALES. 751.

1896    J. McHenry Jones. HEARTS OF GOLD. 343.

1897    *Charles Elmer Waterman. THE PROMISED LAND AND OTHER TALES. 808.

1898    *Paul Laurence Dunbar. FOLKS FROM DIXIE. 753.

_____. THE UNCALLED. 156.

1899    *Charles Waddell Chesnutt. THE CONJURE WOMAN. 741.

*_____. THE WIFE OF HIS YOUTH AND OTHER STORIES OF THE COLOR LINE. 742.

*Alice Ruth Moore (Nelson) Dunbar. THE GOODNESS OF ST. ROCQUE AND OTHER STORIES. 752.

Sutton E. Griggs. IMPERIUM IN IMPERIO. 243.

1900    Charles Waddell Chesnutt. THE HOUSE BEHIND THE CEDARS. 83.

Paul Laurence Dunbar. THE LOVE OF LANDRY. 157.

*_____. THE STRENGTH OF GIDEON AND OTHER STORIES. 754.

Pauline E. Hopkins. CONTENDING FORCES; A ROMANCE ILLUSTRATIVE OF NEGRO LIFE NORTH AND SOUTH. 294.

1901    Charles Waddell Chesnutt. THE MARROW OF TRADITION. 84.

Paul Laurence Dunbar. THE FANATICS. 158.

Sutton E. Griggs. OVERSHADOWED. 244.

Amelia E. Johnson. MARTINA MERIDEN, OR, WHAT IS MY MOTIVE? 329.

1902    *James David Corrothers. THE BLACK CAT CLUB. 746.

Paul Laurence Dunbar. THE SPORT OF THE GODS. 159.

John Stephens Durham. DIANE, PRINCESS OF HAITI. 161.

Charles H. Fowler. HISTORICAL ROMANCE OF THE AMERICAN NEGRO. 198.

Sutton E. Griggs. UNFETTERED, A NOVEL. 245.

Pauline E. Hopkins. WINONA: A TALE OF NEGRO LIFE IN THE SOUTH AND SOUTHWEST. 295.

_____. OF ONE BLOOD; OR, THE HIDDEN SELF. 296.

George Langhorne Pryor. NEITHER BOND NOR FREE. 504.

1903 *Paul Laurence Dunbar. IN OLD PLANTATION DAYS. 755.

*Samuel E. MacDonald. THE OTHER GIRL, WITH SOME FURTHER STORIES AND POEMS. 788.

T.E.D. Nash. LOVE AND VENGEANCE. 448.

1904 Handy Nereus Brown. THE NECROMANCER. 60.

*Paul Laurence Dunbar. THE HEART OF HAPPY HOLLOW. 756.

Henry Theodore Johnson. KEY TO THE PROBLEM. 335.

Edward Augustus Johnson. LIGHT AHEAD FOR THE NEGRO. 332.

1905 Charles Waddell Chesnutt. THE COLONEL'S DREAM. 85.

*Silas Xavier Floyd. FLOYD'S FLOWERS. 761.

Sutton E. Griggs. THE HINDERED HAND; OR, THE REIGN OF THE REPRESSIONIST. 246.

1906 *George McClellan. OLD GREENBOTTOM INN AND OTHER STORIES. 787.

1907 *James Ephraim McGirt. THE TRIUMPHS OF EPHRAIM. 789.

1908 Sutton E. Griggs. POINTING THE WAY. 247.

Henry Davis Middleton. DREAMS OF AN IDLE HOUR. 431.

1909 John Wesley Grant. OUT OF THE DARKNESS; OR, DIABOLISM AND DESTINY. 233.

1910 Thomas H.B. Walker. BEBBLY, OR THE VICTORIOUS PREACHER. 626.

Robert L. Waring. AS WE SEE IT. 635.

1911 W.E.B. DuBois. THE QUEST OF THE SILVER FLEECE. 150.

1912 *Joseph Cotter. NEGRO TALES. 747.

James Weldon Johnson. THE AUTOBIOGRAPHY OF AN EX-COLORED MAN. 337.

Yorke Jones. THE CLIMBERS. 348.

Thomas H.B. Walker. REVELATION, TRIAL AND EXILE OF JOHN IN EPICS. 627.

1913 Oscar Micheaux. THE CONQUEST. 424.

1914 Olivia Ward Bush. DRIFTWOOD. 68.

1915 William Mobile Ashby. REDDER BLOOD. 8.

F. Grant Gilmore. "THE PROBLEM": A MILITARY NOVEL. 211.

Oscar Micheaux. THE FORGED NOTE. 425.

Otis M. Shackelford. LILLIAN SIMMONS. 549.

Thomas H.B. Walker. J. JOHNSON, OR THE UNKNOWN MAN. 628.

1916 *Aaron Eugene Aiken. EXPOSURE OF NEGRO SOCIETY AND SO-CIETIES. . . TWENTY STORIES COMBINED. 729.

John Edward Bruce. THE AWAKENING OF HEZEKIAH JONES. 66.

George McClellan. THE PATH OF DREAMS. 397.

1917 Henry F. Downing. THE AMERICAN CAVALRYMAN. 144.

George Washington Ellis. THE LEOPARD'S CLAW. 167.

Sarah Lee Brown Fleming. HOPE'S HIGHWAY. 191.

Charles Henry Holmes [pseud. Clayton Adams]. ETHIOPIA, THE LAND OF PROMISE. 292.

Oscar Micheaux. THE HOMESTEADER. 426.

J.A. Rogers. FROM "SUPERMAN" TO MAN. 527.

1919 Charlotte Hawkins Brown. "MAMMY," AN APPEAL TO THE HEART OF THE SOUTH. 57.

Herman Dreer. THE IMMEDIATE JEWEL OF HIS SOUL. 145.

Maggie Fullilove. WHO WAS RESPONSIBLE? 199.

Robert Archer Tracy. THE SWORD OF NEMESIS. 599.

1920 *Silas Xavier Floyd. SHORT STORIES FOR COLORED PEOPLE, BOTH OLD AND YOUNG. 762.

*Fenton Johnson. TALES OF DARKEST AMERICA. 781.

Zara Wright. BLACK AND WHITE TANGLED THREADS. 694.

\_\_\_\_\_. KENNETH. 695.

1921    Mary Etta Spencer. THE RESENTMENT. 582.

1922    *Silas Xavier Floyd. THE NEW FLOYD'S FLOWERS. 763.

        *William Pickens. THE VENGEANCE OF THE GODS AND THREE OTHER STORIES OF REAL AMERICAN COLOR LINE LIFE. 799.

        Lillian E. Wood. LET MY PEOPLE GO. 683.

1923    Moses Jordan. THE MEAT MAN. 351.

        Jean Toomer. CANE. 598, 804.

1924    John T. Dorsey. THE LION OF JUDAH. 143.

        Jessie R. Fauset. THERE IS CONFUSION. 179.

        Joshua Henry Jones, Jr. BY SANCTION OF LAW. 344.

        Walter White. THE FIRE IN THE FLINT. 658.

1925    *Silas Xavier Floyd. CHARMING STORIES FOR YOUNG AND OLD. 764.

        Harry F. Liscomb. THE PRINCE OF WASHINGTON SQUARE. 386.

1926    Joshua Arthur Brocket. ZIPPORAH, THE MAID OF MIDIAN. 54.

        *William Pickens. AMERICAN AESOP, NEGRO AND OTHER HUMOR. 800.

        *Eric Walrond. TROPIC DEATH. 807.

1927    Med Bridgeford. GOD'S LAW AND MAN'S. 51.

1928    CONFESSIONS OF A NEGRO PREACHER. 94.

        W.E.B. DuBois. DARK PRINCESS. 151.

        E. Elliott Durant and Cuthbert M. Roach. THE PRINCESS OF NARAGPUR, OR A DAUGHTER OF ALLAH. 160.

        Rudolph Fisher. THE WALLS OF JERICHO. 188.

        Nella Larsen. QUICKSAND. 372.

        Claude McKay. HOME TO HARLEM. 399.

1929    Albert Evander Coleman. THE ROMANTIC ADVENTURES OF ROSY, THE OCTOROON. 88.

        Jessie R. Fauset. PLUM BUN. 180.

        Nella Larsen. PASSING. 373.

Claude McKay. BANJO. 400.

Tom Sanders. HER GOLDEN HOUR. 540.

Wallace Thurman. THE BLACKER THE BERRY. 594.

Jean Toomer. "YORK BEACH." 598A.

1930    Eugene Henry Huffman. "NOW I AM CIVILIZED." 300.

Langston Hughes. NOT WITHOUT LAUGHTER. 301.

Gilbert Lubin. THE PROMISED LAND. 389.

John H. Paynter. FUGITIVES OF THE PEARL. 485.

1931    Arna Bontemps. GOD SENDS SUNDAY. 43.

Jessie R. Fauset. THE CHINABERRY TREE. 181.

William S. Henry. OUT OF WEDLOCK. 270.

Dennis F. Imbert. THE COLORED GENTLEMEN. 314.

George S. Schuyler. BLACK NO MORE. 542.

_____. SLAVES TODAY, A STORY OF LIBERIA. 543.

Charles Elmer Waterman. THE WHITE FAWN: A TALE OF THE LAND OF MOLECHUNKAMUNK. 639.

1932    Countee Cullen. ONE WAY TO HEAVEN. 112.

Victor Daly. NOT ONLY WAR, A STORY OF TWO GREAT CON-FLICTS. 114.

Rudolph Fisher. THE CONJURE MAN DIES. 189.

*Claude McKay. GINGERTOWN. 790.

Wallace Thurman. INFANTS OF THE SPRING. 595.

Wallace Thurman and A.L. Furman. THE INTERNE. 596.

1933    Jessie R. Fauset. COMEDY, AMERICAN STYLE. 182.

John H. Hill. PRINCESS MALAH. 274.

Claude McKay. BANANA BOTTOM. 401.

Ezekiel Harry Miller. THE PROTESTANT. 432.

1934    *Langston Hughes. THE WAYS OF WHITE FOLKS. 773.

Zora Neale Hurston. JONAH'S GOURD VINE. 309.

1935    George Wylie Henderson. OLLIE MISS. 268.

Charles Elmer Waterman. CARIB QUEENS. 640.

1936    Arna Bontemps. BLACK THUNDER. 44.

Arthur Joseph [pseud. John Arthur]. DARK METROPOLIS. 352.

O'Wendell Shaw. GREATER NEED BELOW. 553.

1937    Zora Neale Hurston. THEIR EYES WERE WATCHING GOD. 310.

George Washington Lee. RIVER GEORGE. 377.

Waters Edward Turpin. THESE LOW GROUNDS. 603.

1938    *Paul Laurence Dunbar. THE BEST STORIES OF PAUL LAURENCE DUNBAR. 757.

Mercedes Gilbert. AUNT SARAH'S WOODEN GOD. 210.

George Hamlin Ross. BEYOND THE RIVER: A NOVEL. 533.

Richard Wright. UNCLE TOM'S CHILDREN. 810.

1939    William Attaway. LET ME BREATHE THUNDER. 11.

Arna Bontemps. DRUMS AT DUSK. 45.

Zora Neale Hurston. MOSES, MAN OF THE MOUNTAIN. 311.

Gertrude Pitts. TRAGEDIES OF LIFE. 497.

Anne Scott. GEORGE SAMPSON BRITE. 544.

Waters Edward Turpin. O CANAAN! 604.

1940    *Carlyle W. Garner. IT WASN'T FAIR. 766.

John M. Lee. COUNTER-CLOCKWISE. 379.

Richard Wright. NATIVE SON. 689.

1941    William Attaway. BLOOD ON THE FORGE. 12.

Katherine Campbell Graham. UNDER THE COTTONWOOD. 231.

Oscar Micheaux. THE WIND FROM NOWHERE. 427.

1942    Deaderick Franklin Jenkins. IT WAS NOT MY WORLD. 325.

*George Washington Lee. BEALE STREET SUNDOWN. 786.

Annie Greene Nelson. AFTER THE STORM. 464.

Adam Clayton Powell, Sr. PICKETING HELL. 502.

1943    Ruth Thompson Bernard. WHAT'S WRONG WITH LOTTERY? 35.

Edward Gholson. FROM JERUSALEM TO JERICHO. 207.

Curtis Lucas. FLOUR IS DUSTY. 390.

Carl Offord. THE WHITE FACE. 467.

Thomas E. Roach. VICTOR. 520.

Chancellor Williams. THE RAVEN. 665.

1944    *Corinne Dean. COCOANUT SUITE: STORIES OF THE WEST INDIES. 748.

Wade S. Gray. HER LAST PERFORMANCE. 234.

Oscar Micheaux. THE CASE OF MRS. WINGATE. 428.

Annie Greene Nelson. THE DAWN APPEARS. 465.

1945    Lewis A.H. Caldwell. THE POLICY KING. 74.

Chester Himes. IF HE HOLLERS LET HIM GO. 275.

Odella Phelps Wood. HIGH GROUND. 684.

1946    John Paul Blair. DEMOCRACY REBORN. 38.

Werter L. Gross. THE GOLDEN RECOVERY. 248.

George Wylie Henderson. JULE. 269.

Curtis Lucas. THIRD WARD NEWARK. 391.

Oscar Micheaux. THE STORY OF DOROTHY STANFIELD. 429.

Ann Petry. THE STREET. 489.

Frank Yerby. THE FOXES OF HARROW. 698.

1947    Alden Bland. BEHOLD A CRY. 39.

Chester Himes. LONELY CRUSADE. 276.

Deaderick Franklin Jenkins. LETTERS TO MY SON. 326.

Oscar Micheaux. THE MASQUERADE. 430.

Willard Motley. KNOCK ON ANY DOOR. 443.

Ann Petry. COUNTRY PLACE. 490.

E.M. Rasmussen. THE FIRST NIGHT. 507.

William Smith [pseud. Will Thomas]. GOD IS FOR WHITE FOLKS. 574.

Frank Yerby. THE VIXENS. 699.

1948    Zora Neale Hurston. SERAPH ON THE SUWANEE. 312.

William Gardner Smith. LAST OF THE CONQUERORS. 575.

Dorothy West. THE LIVING IS EASY. 648.

Frank Yerby. THE GOLDEN HAWK. 700.

1949  H.L. Hunter. THE MIRACLES OF THE RED ALTAR CLOTH. 304.
A.Q. Jarrett. BENEATH THE SKY. 322.
Willard W. Savoy. ALIEN LAND. 541.
Frank Yerby. PRIDE'S CASTLE. 701.

1950  Alger Leroy Adams [pseud. Philip B. Kaye]. TAFFY. 1.
William Demby. BEETLECREEK. 135.
*Langston Hughes. SIMPLE SPEAKS HIS MIND. 774.
J. Saunders Redding. STRANGER AND ALONE. 512.
William Gardner Smith. ANGER AT INNOCENCE. 576.
Frank Yerby. FLOODTIDE. 702.

1951  Lloyd L. Brown. IRON CITY. 62.
Owen Dodson. BOY AT THE WINDOW. 142.
Amanda Finch. BACK TRAIL: A NOVELLA OF LOVE IN THE SOUTH. 186.
Earl J. Morris. THE COP. 438.
Willard Motley. WE FISHED ALL NIGHT. 444.
Carl Offord. THE NAKED FEAR. 468.
Sadie Mae Rosebrough. WASTED TRAVAIL. 531.
Allen Pelzer Turner. OAKS OF EDEN. 600.
Frank Yerby. A WOMAN CALLED FANCY. 703.

1952  William Demby. LA SETTIMANA DELLA FEDE. 136.
Dorothy Lee Dickens. BLACK ON THE RAINBOW. 140.
Renee Easterling. A STRANGE WAY HOME. 164.
Ralph Ellison. INVISIBLE MAN. 169.
Chester Himes. CAST THE FIRST STONE. 277.
*Wendell Howard. THE LAST REFUGE OF A SCOUNDREL AND OTHER STORIES. 772.
*Langston Hughes. LAUGHING TO KEEP FROM CRYING. 775.
Arthur Joseph [pseud. John Arthur]. VOLCANO IN OUR MIDST. 353.
Curtis Lucas. SO LOW, SO LONELY. 392.
Thomas E. Roach. SAMSON. 521.

Chancellor Williams. HAVE YOU BEEN TO THE RIVER? 666.

Frank Yerby. THE SARACEN BLADE. 704.

1953   Ethel Nishua Arnold. SHE KNEW NO EVIL. 6.

James Baldwin. GO TELL IT ON THE MOUNTAIN. 14.

Gwendolyn Brooks. MAUDE MARTHA. 55.

*Renee Easterling. GIFTS FROM GOD. TWO STORIES. 758.

William Fisher. THE WAITERS. 190.

*John Wesley Groves, IV. PYRRHIC VICTORY: A COLLECTION OF SHORT STORIES. 767.

Florenz H. Hough. BLACK PARADISE. 298.

*Langston Hughes. SIMPLE TAKES A WIFE. 776.

Mark Kennedy. THE PECKING ORDER. 361.

Curtis Lucas. ANGEL. 393.

_____. FORBIDDEN FRUIT. 394.

Ann Petry. THE NARROWS. 491.

Anne Scott. CASE 999, A CHRISTMAS STORY. 545.

Thelma Wamble. ALL IN THE FAMILY. 630.

Thomas Playfair Ward. THE RIGHT TO LIVE. 632.

Richard Wright. THE OUTSIDER. 690.

Frank Yerby. THE DEVIL'S LAUGHTER. 705.

1954   Greene Buster. BRIGHTER SUN. 69.

Seginald Chantrelle. NOT WITHOUT DUST. 80.

D.R. Corbo, Jr. HARD GROUND. 106.

George Peter Crump, Jr. FROM BONDAGE THEY CAME. 110.

Arthur Diggs. BLACK WOMAN. 141.

Chester Himes. THE THIRD GENERATION. 278.

William H. Jones. THE TRIANGLE'S END. 347.

Elsie Jordan. STRANGE SINNER. 349.

John Oliver Killens. YOUNGBLOOD. 362.

William Gardner Smith. SOUTH STREET. 577.

Charles A. Smythwick, Jr. FALSE MEASURE. 579.

Tomas H. Spence and Eric Heath. MARTIN LARWIN. 581.

Charles L. Tarter. FAMILY OF DESTINY. 590.

Elizabeth West Wallace. SCANDAL AT DAYBREAK. 629.

Thomas Playfair Ward. THE CLUTCHES OF CIRCUMSTANCES. 633.

Walter Wiggins, Jr. DREAMS IN REALITY OF THE UNDERSEA CRAFT. 664.

Richard Wright. SAVAGE HOLIDAY. 691.

Frank Yerby. BENTON'S ROW. 706.

_____. BRIDE OF LIBERTY. 707.

1955 Theodore Brown. THE BAND WILL NOT PLAY DIXIE. 64.

Chester Himes. THE PRIMITIVE. 279.

Lillie Muse Humphrey. AGGIE. 303.

Curtis Lucas. LILA. 395.

Thomas Playfiar Ward. THE TRUTH THAT MAKES MEN FREE. 634.

Frank Yerby. THE TREASURE OF PLEASANT VALLEY. 708.

1956 James Baldwin. GIOVANNI'S ROOM. 15.

Mentis Carrere. MAN IN THE CANE. 76.

*Alice Childress. LIKE ONE OF THE FAMILY. 744.

Clarence L. Cooper, Jr. THE SYNDICATE. (ca. 1956-1960). 98.

Elbert L. Harris. THE ATHENIAN. 257.

W. Leon Sydnor. VERONICA. 588.

Nii A. Vanderpuije. THE COUNTERFEIT CORPSE. 607.

Samuel J. Warner. MADAM PRESIDENT-ELECT. 636.

William B. Woods. LANCASTER TRIPLE THOUSAND. 685.

Frank Yerby. CAPTAIN REBEL. 709.

1957 William Bosworth. THE LONG SEARCH. 46.

Edward Branch. THE HIGH PLACES. 50.

W.E.B. DuBois. THE ORDEAL OF MANSART. 152.

Rubynn M. English. CITIZEN, U.S.A. 170.

Chester Himes. FOR LOVE OF IMABELLE. 280.

*Langston Hughes. SIMPLE STAKES A CLAIM. 777.

W. Warner Jackson. THE BIRTH OF THE MARTYR'S GHOST. 319.

Julian Mayfield. THE HIT. 418.

W. Reginald Montague. OLE MAN MOSE. 435.

Letty M. Shaw. ANGEL MINK. 552.

Herbert Simmons. CORNER BOY. 560.

Waters Edward Turpin. THE ROOTLESS. 605.

Frank Yerby. FAIROAKS. 710.

1958   Edmund O. Austin. THE BLACK CHALLENGE. 13.

Claudia Bellinger. WOLF KITTY. 28.

Fay Liddle Coolidge. BLACK IS WHITE. 97.

Herman Dreer. THE TIE THAT BINDS. 146.

Richard Gibson. A MIRROR FOR MAGISTRATES. 208.

George W. Hodges. SWAMP ANGEL. 291.

Langston Hughes. TAMBOURINES TO GLORY. 302.

Elizabeth Kytle. WILLIE MAE. 370.

Ken Lipscomb. DUKE CASANOVA. 385.

Julian Mayfield. THE LONG NIGHT. 419.

Willard Motley. LET NO MAN WRITE MY EPITAPH. 445.

Clarita C. Pretto. THE LIFE OF AUTUMN HOLLIDAY. 503.

Robert Martin Screen. WE CAN'T RUN AWAY FROM HERE. 548.

Jack Calvert Wells. OUT OF THE DEEP. 646.

Jerome Ardell Williams. THE TIN BOX. 669.

Richard Wright. THE LONG DREAM. 692.

Frank Yerby. THE SERPENT AND THE STAFF. 711.

1959   *Alston Anderson. LOVER MAN. 730.

Frank London Brown. TRUMBULL PARK. 58.

James Nelson Coleman. THE NULL-FREQUENCY IMPULSER. 89.

Douglas Cook. CHOKER'S SON. 95.

Joseph A. Davis. BLACK BONDAGE: A NOVEL OF A DOOMED NEGRO IN TODAY'S SOUTH. 118.

W.E.B. DuBois. MANSART BUILDS A SCHOOL. 153.

*Harold Fenderson. THE PHONY AND OTHER STORIES. 759.

Leon R. Harris. RUN ZEBRA RUN! 259.

*Roy L. Hill. TWO WAYS AND OTHER STORIES. 769.

Chester Himes. THE CRAZY KILL. 281.

_____. THE REAL COOL KILLERS. 282.

*Geoffrey Holder and Tom Harshman. BLACK GODS, GREEN ISLANDS. 771.

Nathaniel Hooks. TOWN ON TRIAL. 293.

James F. Lee. THE VICTIMS. 378.

Paule Marshall. BROWN GIRL, BROWNSTONES. 412.

Freeman Pollard. SEEDS OF TURMOIL. 500.

Valaida Potter. SUNRISE OVER ALABAMA. 501.

G. Henderson Puckett. ONE MORE TOMORROW. 505.

Estella Vaught. VENGEANCE IS MINE. 618.

John B. West. AN EYE FOR AN EYE. 649.

E.H. White [pseud. Lydia Watson]. OUR HOMEWARD WAY. 656.

Philip Wooby. NUDE TO THE MEANING OF TOMORROW. 682.

A.H. Yancey. INTERPOSITIONULIFICATION, WHAT THE NEGRO MAY EXPECT. 697.

Frank Yerby. JARRETT'S JADE. 712.

1960   W.C. Cooke. THE RUNGLESS LADDER. 96.

Clarence L. Cooper, Jr. THE SCENE. 99.

Ella Earls Cotton. QUEEN OF PERSIA. 108.

Joseph Mason Andrew Cox. THE SEARCH. 109.

George Cunningham, Jr. LILY-SKIN LOVER. 113.

Chester Himes. ALL SHOT UP. 283.

_____. THE BIG GOLD DREAM. 284.

Minnie T. Shores. PUBLICANS AND SINNERS. 558.

John B. West. BULLETS ARE MY BUSINESS. 650.

_____. COBRA VENOM. 651.

_____. A TASTE FOR BLOOD. 652.

John A. Williams. THE ANGRY ONES. 670.

Frank Yerby. GILLIAN. 713.

1961   Henry L. Anderson. NO USE CRYIN'. 4.

Robert Deal Broadus. SPOKES FOR THE WHEEL. 53.

Clarence L. Cooper, Jr. WEED. 100.

W.E.B. DuBois. WORLDS OF COLOR. 154.

John T. Farrell. THE NAKED TRUTH. 177.

Frank Hercules. WHERE THE HUMMINGBIRD FLIES. 271.

Chester Himes. PINKTOES (first English language publication). 285.

# Appendix

*Langston Hughes. THE BEST OF SIMPLE. 778.

*Will Anthony Madden. TWO AND ONE. 792.

*Paule Marshall. SOUL CLAP HANDS AND SING. 794.

Julian Mayfield. THE GRAND PARADE. 420.

John B. West. DEATH ON THE ROCKS. 653.

_____. NEVER KILL A COP. 654.

John A. Williams. NIGHT SONG. 671.

Pat Wilson. THE SIGN OF KELOA. 680.

*Richard Wright. EIGHT MEN. 811.

Frank Yerby. THE GARFIELD HONOR. 714.

1962   James Baldwin. ANOTHER COUNTRY. 16.

Mattye Jeanette Brown. THE REIGN OF TERROR. 63.

Dorothy Randle Clinton. THE MADDENING SCAR. 87.

Clarence L. Cooper, Jr. THE DARK MESSENGER. 101.

William Cooper. THANK GOD FOR A SONG. 105.

Paul Crump. BURN, KILLER, BURN! 111.

Samuel R. Delany. THE JEWELS OF APTOR. 122.

Ira Lunan Ferguson. OCEE McRAE, TEXAS. 184.

Edwina Gaines. YOUR PEOPLE ARE MY PEOPLE. 200.

William Melvin Kelley. A DIFFERENT DRUMMER. 356.

Charles Perry. PORTRAIT OF A YOUNG MAN DROWNING. 487.

Herbert Simmons. MAN WALKING ON EGGSHELLS. 561.

Theodosia B. Skinner. ICE CREAM FROM HEAVEN. 563.

Joe Smith. DAGMAR OF GREEN HILLS. 569.

Dave Talbot. THE MUSICAL BRIDE. 589.

Robert L. Teague. THE CLIMATE OF CANDOR. 591.

Peter Voglin. NOW YOU LAY ME DOWN TO SLEEP. 620.

Frank Yerby. GRIFFIN'S WAY. 715.

1963   Clarence L. Cooper, Jr. BLACK! TWO SHORT NOVELS. 102.

Junius Edwards. IF WE MUST DIE. 165.

Chester Himes. UNE AFFAIRE DE VIOL. 286.

*Langston Hughes. SOMETHING IN COMMON AND OTHER STORIES. 779.

Milton W. Janssen. DIVIDED. 321.

John Oliver Killens. AND THEN WE HEARD THE THUNDER. 363.

*Will Anthony Madden. FIVE MORE. 793.

Willie Mays and Jeff Harris. DANGER IN CENTER FIELD. 422.

Gordon Parks. THE LEARNING TREE. 482.

Sadie L. Roberson. KILLER OF THE DREAM. 522.

J.A. Rogers. SHE WALKS IN BEAUTY. 528.

William Gardner Smith. THE STONE FACE. 578.

Moses Peter Wells. THREE ADVENTUROUS MEN. 647.

John A. Williams. SISSIE. 672.

Charles Wright. THE MESSENGER. 686.

1964    Robert E. Boles. THE PEOPLE ONE KNOWS. 40.

Samuel R. Delany. THE TOWERS OF TORON. 123.

John T. Flemister. FURLOUGH FROM HELL, A FANTASY. 192.

Christine Forte [pseud. Christine Forster]. A VIEW FROM THE HILL. 196.

Ernest J. Gaines. CATHERINE CARMIER. 201.

Bill Gunn. ALL THE REST HAVE DIED. 250.

Helen Hunter. MAGNIFICENT WHITE MEN. 305.

Kristin Hunter. GOD BLESS THE CHILD. 306.

Beauregard James. THE ROAD TO BIRMINGHAM. 320.

*William Melvin Kelley. DANCERS ON THE SHORE. 784.

Vyola Therese Lahon. THE BIG LIE. 371.

Arthur Lee Smith. BREAK OF DAWN. 565.

Walter E. Sublette [pseud. S.W. Edwards]. GO NOW IN DARKNESS. 587.

Doris V. Washington. YULAN. 638.

Charles Lewis Webb. SASEBO DIARY. 643.

William West. CORNERED. 655.

Richard L. Williams. PARSON WIGGIN'S SON    678.

Carl T. Wilson. THE HALF CASTE. 679.

Frank Yerby. THE OLD GODS LAUGH. 716.

1965    Alston Anderson. ALL GOD'S CHILDREN. 3.

*James Baldwin. GOING TO MEET THE MAN. 732.

Jesse Moore Battles. SOMEBODY PLEASE HELP ME. 22.

Samuel R. Delany. THE BALLAD OF BETA-2. 124.

_____. CAPTIVES OF THE FLAME. 125.

_____. CITY OF A THOUSAND SUNS. 126.

William Demby. THE CATACOMBS. 137.

Ronald Fair. MANY THOUSAND GONE. 171.

James A. Felton. FRUITS OF ENDURING FAITH. 183.

Carmen Anthony Fiore. THE BARRIER. 187.

Chester Himes. PINKTOES (first American published edition). 285.

_____. COTTON COMES TO HARLEM. 287.

Gallan Horsman. THE NOOSE AND THE SPEAR. 297.

*Langston Hughes. SIMPLE'S UNCLE SAM. 780.

Evelyn Allen Johnson. MY NEIGHBOR'S ISLAND. 334.

Joe Johnson. COURTIN', SPORTIN', AND NON-SUPPORTIN'. 338.

LeRoi Jones. THE SYSTEM OF DANTE'S HELL. 345.

Ralph H. Jones. THE PEPPERPOT MAN. 346.

William Melvin Kelley. A DROP OF PATIENCE. 357.

Chester Martin. HE WAS BORN, HE DIED AND HE LIVED. 414.

_____. MIDDLE YEARS (ca. 1965). 415.

Roi Ottley. WHITE MARBLE LADY. 479.

James E. Paulding. SOMETIME TOMORROW. 484.

Hari Rhodes. A CHOSEN FEW. 518.

J. Terry Robinson. WHITE HORSE IN HARLEM. 524.

Lamen Rollins. THE HUMAN RACE A GANG. 530.

Henry Van Dyke. LADIES OF THE RACHMANINOFF EYES. 608.

Richard Wright. "Five Episodes from an Unfinished Novel." 692A.

Frank Yerby. AN ODOR OF SANCTITY. 717.

1966    Nathan Barrett. BARS OF ADAMANT: A TROPICAL NOVEL. 20.

Hal Bennett. A WILDERNESS OF VINES. 30.

Granby Blackwood. UN SANG MAL MELE. 37.

Mentis Carrere. IT'S ALL SOUTH. 77.

John L. Cooper. OPUS ONE. 104.

Charles Davis. TWO WEEKS TO FIND A KILLER. 115.

Samuel R. Delany. BABEL-17. 127.

_____. EMPIRE STAR. 128.

Ronald Fair. HOG BUTCHER. 172.

Christine Forte [pseud. Christine Forster]. YOUNG TIM O'HARA. 197.

Rosa Guy. BIRD AT MY WINDOW. 251.

Chester Himes. THE HEAT'S ON. 288.

_____. RUN MAN RUN. 289.

Kristin Hunter. THE LANDLORD. 307.

Richard B. Koiner. JACK BE QUICK. 369.

Willard Motley. LET NOON BE FAIR. 446.

Jane Phillips. MOJO HAND. 495.

Minnie T. Shores. AMERICANS IN AMERICA. 559.

*Lionel O. Thornhill. THE HUGH STEEL BOLT AND OTHER STORIES AND POEMS. 803.

Lester W. Thorup. CAME THE HARVEST. 593.

*Melvin Van Peebles. LE CHINOIS DU XIVe. 805.

Claude Walker, Jr. SABIH. 623.

Margaret Walker. JUBILEE. 625.

Charles Wright. THE WIG, A MIRROR IMAGE. 687.

1967   Robert Beck [pseud. Iceberg Slim]. TRICK BABY. 24.

James Nelson Coleman. SEEKER FROM THE STARS. 90.

Clarence L. Cooper, Jr. THE FARM. 103.

Samuel R. Delany. THE EINSTEIN INTERSECTION. 129.

Ernest J. Gaines. OF LOVE AND DUST. 202.

Frank Hercules. I WANT A BLACK DOLL. 272.

J. Denis Jackson [pseud. Julian Moreau]. THE BLACK COMMANDOS. 318.

William M. Johnson. THE HOUSE ON CORBETT STREET. 340.

*LeRoi Jones. TALES. 783.

William Melvin Kelley. DEM. 358.

John Oliver Killens. 'SIPPI. 364.

Paul Kirk. NO NEED TO CRY. 368.

Clarence R. Parrish. IMAGES OF DEMOCRACY. 483.

Carlene Hatcher Polite. THE FLAGELLANTS. 498.

Leroy L. Ramsey. THE TRIAL AND THE FIRE. 506.

Ishmael Reed. THE FREE-LANCE PALLBEARERS. 513.

Bryant Rollins. DANGER SONG. 529.

Melvin Van Peebles. LE PERMISSION. 611.

Roberta B. Watson. CLOSED DOORS. 642.

John Edgar Wideman. A GLANCE AWAY. 661.

John A. Williams. THE MAN WHO CRIED I AM. 673.

Frank Yerby. GOAT SONG. 718.

1968  James Baldwin. TELL ME HOW LONG THE TRAIN'S BEEN GONE. 17.

Hal Bennett. THE BLACK WINE. 31.

Robert E. Boles. CURLING. 41.

Samuel R. Delany. NOVA. 130.

*Ernest J. Gaines. BLOODLINE. 765.

Nathan C. Heard. HOWARD STREET. 264.

Audrey Lee. THE CLARION PEOPLE. 375.

C.T. Morrison. THE FLAME IN THE ICEBOX. 439.

Bernard S. Smith. BORN FOR MALICE. 566.

Maurice L. Smith. WHO CARES. 571.

Melvin Van Peebles. A BEAR FOR THE FBI. 612.

Alyce R. Warren. INTO THESE DEPTHS. 637.

Jim E. Whitney. WAYWARD O'ER TUNER SHEFFARD. 660.

Frank Yerby. JUDAS, MY BROTHER: THE STORY OF THE THIRTEENTH DISCIPLE. 719.

1969  *Arthenia J. Bates. SEEDS BENEATH THE SNOW: VIGNETTES FROM THE SOUTH. 734.

Robert Beck [pseud. Iceberg Slim]. MAMA BLACK WIDOW. 25.

Barry Beckham. MY MAIN MOTHER. 26.

Cecil Brown. THE LIFE AND LOVES OF MR. JIVEASS NIGGER. 56.

Frank London Brown. THE MYTH MAKER. 59.

Steve Cannon. GROOVE, BANG AND JIVE AROUND. 75.

Grimaldo Carvalho. THE NEGRO MESSIAH. 79.

Merton H. Coleman. THAT GODLESS WOMAN. 91.

Clarence Farmer. SOUL ON FIRE. 176.

Ira Lunan Ferguson. THE BIOGRAPHY OF G. WASH CARTER, WHITE. 185.

*_____. WHICH ONE OF YOU IS INTERRACIAL? AND OTHER STORIES. 760.

Herman Cromwell Gilbert. THE UNCERTAIN SOUND. 209.

Sam Greenlee. THE SPOOK WHO SAT BY THE DOOR. 241.

Chester Himes. BLIND MAN WITH A PISTOL. 290.

Hubert E. Johnson and Loretta Johnson. POPPY. 336.

John Oliver Killens. SLAVES. 365.

Jess Kimbrough. DEFENDER OF THE ANGELS. 367.

Audrey Lee. THE WORKERS. 376.

William Mahoney. BLACK JACOB. 404.

Clarence Major. ALL-NIGHT VISITORS. 405.

Paule Marshall. THE CHOSEN PLACE, THE TIMELESS PEOPLE. 413.

*James Alan McPherson. HUE AND CRY. 791.

Robert Deane Pharr. THE BOOK OF NUMBERS. 492.

Ishmael Reed. YELLOW BACK RADIO BROKE-DOWN. 514.

Rose Robinson. EAGLE IN THE AIR. 526.

Rawle Simpson. ADVENTURES INTO THE UNKNOWN. 562.

Raymond Spence. NOTHING BLACK BUT A CADILLAC. 580.

Henry Van Dyke. BLOOD OF STRAWBERRIES. 609.

Berta Verne. ELASTIC FINGERS. 619.

Thelma Wamble. LOOK OVER MY SHOULDER. 631.

Edward G. Williams. NOT LIKE NIGGERS. 668.

John A. Williams. SONS OF DARKNESS, SONS OF LIGHT. 674.

*Richie Worlds. FOUR YEARS AS A NUN AND OTHER STORIES. 809.

Sara E. Wright. THIS CHILD'S GONNA LIVE. 693.

Frank Yerby. SPEAK NOW. 720.

1970   Sol Battle. MELANGE IN BLACK. 21.

Hal Bennett. LORD OF DARK PLACES. 32.

Odessa Bond. THE DOUBLE TRAGEDY. 42.

George Cain. BLUESCHILD BABY. 72.

# Appendix

Lular L. Carson. THE PRICELESS GIFT. 78.

*Cyrus Colter. THE BEACH UMBRELLA. 745.

Samuel R. Delany. THE FALL OF THE TOWERS. 131.

*Henry Dumas. ARK OF BONES AND OTHER STORIES. 750.

Ronald Fair. WORLD OF NOTHING: TWO NOVELLAS. 173.

Ruth A. Fairley. ROCKS AND ROSES. 175.

Madeleine Sophie Gary. VIGNETTES OF THE BEAM IN A NIGGER'S EYE. 205.

Joe Greene [pseud. B.B. Johnson]. SUPERSPADE NO. 1: DEATH OF A BLUE-EYED SOUL BROTHER. 235.

_____ [pseud. B.B. Johnson]. SUPERSPADE NO. 2: BLACK IS BEAUTIFUL. 236.

_____ [pseud. B.B. Johnson]. SUPERSPADE NO. 3: THAT'S WHERE THE CAT'S AT, BABY. 237.

_____ [pseud. B.B. Johnson]. SUPERSPADE NO. 4: MOTHER OF THE YEAR. 238.

_____ [pseud. B.B. Johnson]. SUPERSPADE NO. 5: BAD DAY FOR A BLACK BROTHER. 239.

John Wesley Groves, IV. SHELLBREAK. 249.

Emma Lou Jackson. THE VEIL OF NANCY. 317.

Hawke Jarry. BLACK SCHOOLMASTER. 323.

William Melvin Kelley. DUNFORDS TRAVELS EVERYWHERES. 359.

Louise Meriwether. DADDY WAS A NUMBER RUNNER. 423.

Toni Morrison. THE BLUEST EYE. 440.

J. Terry Robinson. THE DOUBLE CIRCLE PEOPLE. 525.

A. Bertrand Royal. WHICH WAY TO HEAVEN? 534.

George B. Russ. OVER EDOM, I LOST MY SHOE. 536.

Gil Scott-Heron. THE VULTURE. 546.

George Lawson Smith. TRANSFER. 568.

Chuck Stone. KING STRUT. 585.

Peter Turner. BLACK HEAT. 601.

Mae Caesar Turnor. UNCLE EZRA HOLDS PRAYER MEETING IN THE WHITE HOUSE. 602.

Alice Walker. THE THIRD LIFE OF GRANGE COPELAND. 621.

Thomas J. White. TO HELL AND BACK AT 16. 657.

John Edgar Wideman. HURRY HOME. 662.

Al Young.  SNAKES.  726.

1971    Russell Atkins.  MALEFICIUM.  10.

*Ed Bullins.  THE HUNGERED ONE.  737.

George Davis.  COMING HOME.  117.

Nolan Davis.  SIX BLACK HORSES.  119.

*Samuel R. Delany.  DRIFTGLASS.  749.

Ernest J. Gaines.  THE AUTOBIOGRAPHY OF MISS JANE PITTMAN.  203.

Donald Goines.  DOPEFIEND, THE STORY OF A BLACK JUNKIE.  215.

Joe Greene [pseud. B.B. Johnson].  SUPERSPADE NO. 6:  BLUES FOR A BLACK SISTER.  240.

LeRoi Rossetti Haskins.  THE WEAK ARM OF JUSTICE.  261.

*Samuel M. Johnson.  OFTEN BACK: THE TALES OF HARLEM.  782.

June Jordan.  HIS OWN WHERE.  350.

John Oliver Killens.  THE COTILLION, OR ONE GOOD BULL IS HALF THE HERD.  366.

A.C. McWhortle.  LENA.  403.

B.J. Mason.  THE JERUSALEM FREEDOM MANUFACTURING CO.  416.

*Horace Mungin.  HOW MANY NIGGERS MAKE HALF A DOZEN.  796.

*Ann Petry.  MISS MURIEL AND OTHER STORIES.  798.

Robert Deane Pharr.  S.R.O.  493.

Carl L. Shears.  NIGGERS AND PO' WHITE TRASH.  554.

Daniel Smith.  A WALK IN THE CITY.  567.

Odessa Smith.  THE FLAME.  572.

John Stewart.  LAST COOL DAYS.  584.

Henry Van Dyke.  DEAD PIANO.  610.

Melvin Van Peebles.  SWEET SWEETBACK'S BAADASSSSS SONG.  613.

Drake Walker.  BUCK AND THE PREACHER.  624.

James Wylie.  THE LOST REBELLION.  696.

Frank Yerby.  THE DAHOMEAN, AN HISTORICAL NOVEL.  721.

1972    *Toni Cade Bambara (Toni Cade).  GORILLA, MY LOVE AND OTHER STORIES.  733.

# Appendix

Barry Beckham. RUNNER MACK. 27.

Cyrus Colter. THE RIVER OF EROS. 92.

Donald J. Cotton. SORE FOOTS. 107.

Charles W. Davis. THE NUT AND BOLT. 116.

Ronald Fair. WE CAN'T BREATHE. 174.

Donald Goines. WHORESON, THE STORY OF A GHETTO PIMP. 216.

_____. BLACK GANGSTER. 217.

Odie Hawkins. GHETTO SKETCHES. 263.

Nathan C. Heard. TO REACH A DREAM. 265.

Arnold Kemp. EAT OF ME, I AM THE SAVIOR. 360.

Julius Lester. TWO LOVE STORIES. 383.

D.C. Love. THE SHERIFF. 387.

Arthur Lubin. WAMPALA ON THE HUDSON. 388.

William P. McKenzie. THE SOLEMN HOUR. 402.

Cleo Overstreet. THE BOAR HOG WOMAN. 480.

Ishmael Reed. MUMBO JUMBO. 515.

Gil Scott-Heron. THE NIGGER FACTORY. 547.

Theodosia B. Skinner. DILEMMA OF A COLLEGE GIRL. 564.

Melvin Van Peebles. DON'T PLAY US CHEAP. 614.

Bill Webster. ONE BY ONE. 645.

John A. Williams. CAPTAIN BLACKMAN. 675.

Frank Yerby. THE GIRL FROM STORYVILLE. 722.

1973   Martin Ashley. CHECKMATE AND DEATHMATE. 9.

*Wally Bohanon. WALLY BOHANON: HIS SHORT STORIES. 735.

*Arna Bontemps. THE OLD SOUTH: "A SUMMER TRAGEDY" AND OTHER STORIES OF THE THIRTIES. 736.

Lawrance Briscoe. FISHER'S ALLEY. 52.

Josephine Stephens Brown. THE WAY OF THE SHADOWS. 61.

Ed Bullins. THE RELUCTANT RAPIST. 67.

Johnnie Mae Cain. WHITE BASTARDS. 73.

Cyrus Colter. THE HIPPODROME. 93.

John Dee. STAGGER LEE. 120.

Samuel R. Delany. THE TIDES OF LUST. 132.

Mary Drummond. COME GO WITH ME. 147.

Teresa Ellis. NO WAY BACK: A NOVELLA. 168.

Leon Forrest. THERE IS A TREE MORE ANCIENT THAN EDEN. 194.

Donald Goines. STREET PLAYERS. 218.

_____. WHITE MAN'S JUSTICE, BLACK MAN'S GRIEF. 219.

_____. BLACK GIRL LOST. 220.

James L. Harris. ENDURANCE. 258.

Christine Hathorn. THE UNDOING OF MISS ABAGAIL WRIGLEY. 262.

*Chester Himes. BLACK ON BLACK: BABY SISTER AND SELECTED WRITINGS. 770.

Blyden Jackson. OPERATION BURNING CANDLE. 315.

Ronald Lewis. THE·LAST JUNKIE. 384.

Clarence Major. NO. 406.

Roosevelt Mallory. RADCLIFF, NO. 1: HARLEM HIT. 408.

Loften Mitchell. THE STUBBORN OLD LADY WHO RESISTED CHANGE. 434.

Toni Morrison. SULA. 441.

Joseph Nazel. MY NAME IS BLACK! 449.

Jon Palmer. HOUSE FULL OF BROTHERS. 481.

Carl L. Shears [pseud. Saggittarus]. THE COUNT-DOWN TO BLACK GENOCIDE. 555.

Lois A. Smith [pseud. Jezebelle]. THE MOST PRECIOUS MOMENTS. 570.

Bert Underwood. A BRANCH OF VELVET. 606.

Melvin Van Peebles. AIN'T SUPPOSED TO DIE A NATURAL DEATH. 615.

*Alice Walker. IN LOVE AND TROUBLE: STORIES OF BLACK WOMEN. 806.

John Edgar Wideman. THE LYNCHERS. 663.

Dennis A. Williams and Spero Pines. THEM THAT'S NOT. 667.

Charles Wright. ABSOLUTELY NOTHING TO GET ALARMED ABOUT. 688.

1974    James Baldwin. IF BEALE STREET COULD TALK. 18.

Hal Bennett. WAIT UNTIL THE EVENING. 33.

# Appendix

*Charles W[addell]. Chesnutt. THE SHORT FICTION OF CHARLES W. CHESNUTT. 743.

Shirley Graham DuBois. ZULU HEART. 149.

Nivi-Kofi A. Easley. THE MILITANTS. 163.

Beatrice Garrett. WELFARE ON SKID ROW. 204.

Donald Goines. ELDORADO RED. 221.

_____. SWAMP MAN. 222.

_____. NEVER DIE ALONE. 223.

_____ [pseud. Al C. Clark]. CRIME PARTNERS. 224.

_____ [pseud. Al C. Clark]. DEATH LIST. 225.

_____. DADDY COOL. 226.

_____ [pseud. Al C. Clark]. CRY REVENGE! 227.

Willie Hagan. THE BLACK TARNISHED IMAGE. 253.

Nathan C. Heard. A COLD FIRE BURNING. 266.

Calvin Hernton. SCARECROW. 273.

Charles Johnson. FAITH AND THE GOOD THING. 331.

Mack Leonard. COVER MY REAR. 380.

John McCluskey. LOOK WHAT THEY DONE TO MY SONG. 398.

Roosevelt Mallory. RADCLIFF, No. 2: SAN FRANCISCO VENDETTA. 409.

Alison Mills. FRANCISCO. 433.

Albert Murray. TRAIN WHISTLE GUITAR. 447.

Joseph Nazel. THE BLACK EXORCIST. 450.

_____. BLACK IS BACK. 451.

_____. THE ICEMAN, NO. 1: BILLION DOLLAR DEATH. 452.

_____. THE ICEMAN, NO. 2: THE GOLDEN SHAFT. 453.

_____. THE ICEMAN, NO. 3: SLICK REVENGE. 454.

_____. THE ICEMAN, NO. 4: SUNDAY FIX. 455.

_____. THE ICEMAN, NO. 5: SPINNING TARGET. 456.

_____. THE ICEMAN, NO. 6: CANADIAN KILL. 457.

Marc Olden. BLACK SAMURAI. 469.

_____. BLACK SAMURAI, NO. 2: GOLDEN KILL. 470.

_____. BLACK SAMURAI, NO. 3: KILLER WARRIOR. 471.

_____. BLACK SAMURAI, NO. 4: THE DEADLY PEARL. 472.

_____. BLACK SAMURAI, NO. 5: THE INQUISITION. 473.

Richard Perry. CHANGES. 488.

James-Howard Readus. THE DEATH MERCHANTS. 508.

Ishmael Reed. THE LAST DAYS OF LOUISIANA RED. 516.

Fran Ross. OREO. 532.

Carl L. Shears [pseud. Saggittarus]. BEFORE THE SETTING SUN: THE AGE BEFORE HAMBONE. 556.

Ann Allen Shockley. LOVING HER. 557.

Vern E. Smith. THE JONES MEN. 573.

Frank Yerby. THE VOYAGE UNPLANNED. 723.

1975   Timothy L. Bottoms. MR. SCHUTZER. 47.

David Bradley. SOUTH STREET. 49.

*Clifton Bullock. BABY CHOCOLATE AND OTHER SHORT STORIES. 738.

Reggie Byer. NOBODY GETS RICH. 71.

Samuel R. Delany. DHALGREN. 133.

Blanche Faulkner. THE LIVELY HOUSE. 178.

Kathlyn Gay and Ben E. Barnes. THE RIVER FLOWS BACKWARDS. 206.

Donald Goines [pseud. Al C. Clark]. KENYATTA'S ESCAPE. 228.

_____ [pseud. Al C. Clark]. KENYATTA'S LAST HIT. 229.

_____. INNER CITY HOODLUM. 230.

Marcus A. Hart. THE LOVER WITH A KILLER'S INSTINCT. 260.

*Jerry Herman. AND DEATH WON'T COME: THREE SHORT STORIES. 768.

Kristin Hunter. THE SURVIVORS. 308.

Blyden Jackson. TOTEM. 316.

Eugene D. Johnson. OF HUMAN KINDNESS. 333.

Gayl Jones. CORREGIDORA. 341.

Mack Leonard. FROM LOVE TO LOVE. 381.

Clarence Major. REFLEX AND BONE STRUCTURE. 407.

Roosevelt Mallory. RADCLIFF, NO. 3: DOUBLE TROUBLE. 410.

James A. Mays. MERCY IS KING. 421.

Marie E. Moore. LITTLE WHITE SHOES. 436.

Joseph Nazel. THE BLACK GESTAPO. 459.

_____. DEATH FOR HIRE. 460.

_____. THE ICEMAN, NO. 7: THE SHAKEDOWN. 458.

_____ [pseud. Dom Gober]. KILLER COP. 461.

Marc Olden. BLACK SAMURAI, NO. 6: THE WARLOCK. 474.

_____. BLACK SAMURAI, NO. 7: SWORD OF ALLAH. 475.

_____. BLACK SAMURAI, NO. 8: THE KATANA. 476.

Robert Deane Pharr. THE SOUL MURDER CASE: A CONFESSION OF THE VICTIM. 494.

Carlene Hatcher Polite. SISTER X AND THE VICTIMS OF FOUL PLAY. 499.

James-Howard Readus. THE BLACK ASSASSIN. 510.

_____. THE BIG HIT. 509.

Arthur Robinson. HANG THAT NIGGER. 523.

Christopher Rudolph. THE BOY WHO CURSED GOD. 535.

Frank Shackleford. OLD ROCKING CHAIR. 550.

Herman Stampede. OF MELANCHOLY MALE. 583.

*John Stewart. CURVING ROAD: STORIES. 802.

Carolyn Tillman. LIFE ON WHEELS. 597.

John A. Williams. MOTHERSILL AND THE FOXES. 676.

Bily Wms-Forde. REQUIEM FOR A BLACK AMERICAN CAPITALIST. 681.

Frank Yerby. TOBIAS AND THE ANGEL. 724.

Al Young. WHO IS ANGELINA? 727.

1976    *Mignon Holland Anderson. MOSTLY WOMENFOLK AND A MAN OR TWO. 731.

Mattie Beason. WEST TO THE OHIO RIVER. 23.

Hal Bennett. SEVENTH HEAVEN. 34.

J.M. Boullon. SURRENDER THE DREAM. 48.

Octavia E. Butler. PATTERNMASTER. 70.

Kiarri Cheatwood. LIGHTNING IN THE SWAMP. 81.

Samuel R. Delany. TRITON. 134.

Al Dickens. UNCLE YAH YAH. 139.

David Graham DuBois. . . .AND BID HIM SING. 148.

Henry Dumas. JONOAH AND THE GREEN STONE. 155.

J. Lance Gilmore. HELL HAS NO EXIT. 212.

James P. Girard. CHANGING ALL THOSE CHANGES. 213.

Sam Greenlee. BAGHDAD BLUES. 242.

Rosa Guy. RUBY. 252.

Charlie Avery Harris. MACKING GANGSTER. 255.

_____. WHOREDAUGHTER. 256.

Roland S. Jefferson. THE SCHOOL ON 103RD STREET. 324.

Gayl Jones. EVA'S MAN. 342.

*Yusef Lateef. SPHERES. 785.

William Lawson. ZEPPELIN COMING DOWN. 374.

Mack Leonard. ANOTHER FRONT: A NOVEL OF WORLD WAR II. 382.

Charles Lyons [pseud. Is Said]. STREET JUSTICE. 396.

Roosevelt Mallory. RADCLIFF, NO. 4: NEW JERSEY SHOWDOWN. 411.

Joseph Nazel. BLACK FURY. 462.

_____. BLACK PROPHET. 463.

Leon Thomas Newton. VERITUS, THE NIRVANA FROM THE EAST. 466.

Marc Olden. HARKER FILE, NO. 1. 477.

_____. HARKER FILE, NO. 2: DEAD AND PAID FOR. 478.

James-Howard Readus. BLACK RENEGADES. 511.

Ishmael Reed. FLIGHT TO CANADA. 517.

Ntozake Shange. SASSAFRASS: A NOVELLA. 551.

Melvin Van Peebles. JUST AN OLD SWEET SONG. 616.

_____. THE TRUE AMERICAN: A FOLK FABLE. 617.

Alice Walker. MERIDIAN. 622.

John A. Williams. THE JUNIOR BACHELOR SOCIETY. 677.

Frank Yerby. A ROSE FOR ANA MARIA. 725.

Al Young. SITTING PRETTY. 728.

1977　Toni Morrison. SONG OF SOLOMON. 442.

# AUTHOR INDEX

This index includes all authors, editors, and other contributors cited in the text. Numbers refer to entry numbers. This index is alphabetized letter by letter.

## A

Abcarian, Richard 882
Adams, Alger Leroy (pseud. Philip B. Kaye) 1, 354
Adams, Clayton. See Holmes, Charles Henry
Adams, George R. 924
Adoff, Arnold 812
Aiken, Aaron Eugene 729
Allen, Samuel W. 1101
Ambler, Madge 1027
Anderson, Alston 3, 730
Anderson, Henry L. 4
Anderson, Mignon Holland 731
Anderson, William H. [pseud. Sanda] 8, 539, 586
Andrews, William L. 828-29, 835-37
Arata, Esther Spring 1089
Arnold, Ethel Nishua 6
Arthur, John. See Joseph, Arthur
Ashby, William Mobile 8
Ashley, Martin 9
Atkins, Russell 10
Attaway, William 11-12, 1152
Austin, Edmund O. 13

## B

Babour, James 1052

Baily, Lugene 944, 949
Baker, Houston A., Jr. 883, 1000, 1028, 1102
Bakish, David 884-85, 908
Baldwin, James 14-20, 732, 883, 886-87, 955, 966, 967, 969, 972, 973, 987, 1000, 1074, 1104, 1118, 1119, 1129, 1133, 1134, 1136, 1152, 1157, 1164
Bambara, Toni Cade 733, 740, 813
Barbour, James 830
Barnes, Ben E. 206
Barrett, Nathan 20
Bates, Arthenia J. 734
Battle, Sol 21
Battles, Jesse Moore 22
Baumbach, Jonathan 1120
Bayliss, John F. 1111
Beards, Richard 1001
Beason, Mattie 23
Beauford, Fred 1029
Beck, Robert [pseud. Iceberg Slim] 25, 313
Beckham, Barry 26-27
Bell, Bernard W. 1103
Bellamy, Joe David 1037
Bellinger, Claudia 28
Bellow, Saul 954
Benjamin, R.C.O. 29
Bennett, Hal 30-34
Benoit, Bernard 945

# Author Index

Benson, Joseph  878
Benston, Kimberly  974
Bernard, Ruth Thompson  35
Berry, Faith  897
Bigsby, C.W.E.  1104
Bischoff, Joan  1039
Blackburn, Sara  1040
Blackson, Lorenzo D.  36
Blackwood, Granby  37
Blair, John Paul  38
Bland, Alden  39
Bohanon, Wally  735
Boles, Robert E.  40–41
Bond, Odessa  42
Bone, Robert A.  838–39, 848–49, 853, 861–62, 883, 888, 926, 934–35, 959, 966, 970, 1054–55, 1106–7, 1120, 1133, 1137
Bontemps, Arna  43–45, 736, 850, 853, 1101, 1105, 1137, 1156
Bosworth, William  46
Bottoms, Timothy L.  47
Boullon, J.M.  48
Bradley, David  49
Braithwaite, Edward  976
Branch, Edward  50, 1101
Brawley, Benjamin  1108
Bridgeford, Med  51
Brignano, Russell Carl  871, 889
Briscoe, Lawrance  52
Britt, David D.  840
Broadus, Robert Deal  53
Brocket, Joshua Arthur  54
Bronz, Stephen H.  1109
Brooks, Gwendolyn  55, 1102
Brown, Cecil M.  56, 897, 1123
Brown, Charlotte Hawkins  57
Brown, Frank London  58–59
Brown, Handy Nereus  60
Brown, Josephine Stephens  61
Brown, Lloyd L.  62, 1110–11
Brown, Lloyd W.  950, 977
Brown, Mattye Jeanette  63
Brown, Sterling A.  1112–14
Brown, Theodore  64
Brown, William Wells  65, 1052
Browne, W. Francis  986
Bruce, John Edward  66
Bryant, Jerry H.  987, 1014–15, 1030

Bryer, Jackson R.  872, 1071
Bullins, Ed  67, 737, 1157
Bullock, Clifton  738
Burgess, M.L.  739
Burke, William M.  988, 1016
Bush, Olivia Ward  68
Buster, Greene  69
Butcher, Margaret  1115
Butler, Octavia E.  70
Byer, Reggie  71

## C

Cade, Toni.  See Bambara, Toni Cade
Cain, George  72, 1102, 1123
Cain, Johnnie Mae  73
Caldwell, Lewis A.  74
Calverton, V.F.  1116
Cannon, Steve  75
Carrere, Mentis  76–77
Carson, Lular L.  78
Carter, Tom  1017
Carvalho, Grimaldo  79
Cash, Earl A.  989
Cayton, Horace R.  897, 936, 1137
Chandler, Sue P.  1091
Chantrelle, Seginald  80
Chapman, Abraham  1056, 1111, 1117
Chaw, O'Wendell  553
Cheatwood, Kiarri  81
Chesnut, Robert  82, 98
Chesnutt, Charles Waddell  83–85, 430, 741–43, 830, 831A, 833, 839, 841, 1052, 1119, 1136
Chester, Alfred  949A
Childress, Alice  744, 984
Clark, Al C.  See Goines, Donald
Clarke, John Henrik  814–15, 949, 1101
Cleaver, Eldridge  967, 970, 1123
Clinton, Dorothy Randle  87
Clipper, Lawrence J.  950
Coleman, Albert Evander  88
Coleman, James Nelson  89–90
Coleman, Merton H.  91
Collier, Eugenia W.  949
Colter, Cyrus  92–93, 745, 1156, 1157

134

# Author Index

## F

Fabre, Michel  875, 881, 891-92, 898, 906, 909, 945, 970, 1120
Faggett, H.L.  817, 818
Fair, Ronald  171-74
Fairley, Ruth A.  175
Farmer, Clarence  176
Farnsworth, Robert M.  899, 1104
Farrell, John T.  177
Farrison, Edward W.  854
Farrison, William Edward  972
Faulkner, Blanche  178
Faulkner, Howard  1003
Fauset, Jessie R.  179-82, 1105, 1136
Felton, James A.  183
Fenderson, Harold  759
Fenderson, Lewis H.  1032
Ferguson, Ira Lunan  184-85, 760
Fiedler, Leslie A.  1133
Finch, Amanda  186
Fiore, Carmen Anthony  187
Fischer, Russell G.  961
Fishburn, Katherine  892A
Fisher, Rudolph  188-89, 1105, 1167
Fisher, William  190
Fisk University  832
Fleming, Robert E.  830, 990, 1052
Fleming, Sarah Lee Brown  191
Flemister, John T.  192
Floyd, Silas Xavier  761-64
Ford, Nick Aaron  817, 818, 949, 1033, 1111, 1124
Forget-Me-Not. See Kelley, Emma Dunham
Forrest, Leon  194
Forster, Christine. See Forte, Christine
Forte, Christine [pseud. Christine Forster]  195, 196-97
Fortenberry, George  1074, 1164
Fowler, Charles H.  198
Frank, Waldo  853
Freenay, Mildred  832
French, Warren  1104
French, William P.  1063
Friedman, Alan  1034
Fuller, Edmund  939
Fuller, Hoyt W.  909, 910, 1104, 1128

Fullilove, Maggie  199
Furman, A.L.  596

## G

Gaines, Edwina  200
Gaines, Ernest J.  201-3, 765, 1025, 1156, 1157
Garner, Carlyle W.  766
Garrett, Beatrice  204
Gary, Madeleine Sophie  205
Gay, Kathlyn  206
Gayle, Addison, Jr.  843, 863, 897, 927, 953, 969, 1004, 1019, 1125-28
Georgakas, Dan  992
Gerard, Albert  1129
Gholson, Edward  207
Gibson, Donald B.  874, 876, 877, 883, 890, 902, 905, 948, 958, 962, 972, 1130
Gibson, Richard  208
Giddings, Paula  978
Gilbert, Herman Cromwell  209
Gilbert, Mercedes  210
Gilman, Richard  1104, 1131
Gilmore, F. Grant  211
Gilmore, J. Lance  212
Girard, James P.  213
Glicksberg, Charles I.  959
Gloster, Hugh M.  853, 1066, 1132
Gober, Dom. See Nazel, Joseph
Goines, Donald [pseud. Al C. Clark]  215-30
Gottesman, Ronald  953A
Graham, Katherine Campbell  231
Graham, Shirley. See DuBois, Shirley Graham
Grant, John Wesley  233
Grant, Liz  1042
Gray, Wade S.  234
Greene, Joe [pseud. B.B. Johnson]  235-40, 330
Greenlee, Sam  241-42
Griffin, John C.  847
Griggs, Sutton E[lbert].  243-47, 1052, 1136
Gross, Seymour L.  1133
Gross, Theodore L.  1104, 1134

# Author Index

# Author Index

# Author Index

# TITLE INDEX

This index includes all titles of books which are cited in the text. Titles of articles are not included. In some cases, lengthy titles have been shortened. Numbers refer to entry numbers. This index is alphabetized letter by letter.

# Title Index

# Title Index

# SUBJECT INDEX

This index is alphabetized letter by letter. Underlined entry numbers refer to main areas within the subject.

# Subject Index

Conference of Negro Writers, First
(1959) 1101
Cook, Mercer A. 1111
Corry, John 949
CRISIS (periodical) 1155
Cullen, Countee 1109, 1166

## D

Dahomey in fiction 721
Davis, Arthur P. 1101, 1133
Delany, Martin R. 1052
Demby, William 934–43, 1152, 1156
Detective fiction, critical studies of
916, 920
Dickens, Charles 918
Dickstein, Morris 898
Dodson, Owen 1156
Drama, Afro-American, critical
studies of 1112
DuBois, W.E.B. 853
Dunbar, Paul Laurence 1052, 1102,
1136

## E

Ellison, Ralph 877, 944–60, 962,
982, 994, 1071, 1974,
1102, 1104, 1118-19,
1123, 1129-30, 1133-36,
1152, 1156, 1159
Emanuel, James A. 897, 1111
Ethiopia in fiction 292
Existential fiction 902, 905, 934,
1129
architectural imagery and 974
Experimental fiction 1038

## F

Fabre, Michel 898, 909, 970,
1120
Farce 1034
Farnsworth, Robert 1104
Farrison, William Edward 972
Faulkner, William 1001, 1003, 1005
Fauset, Jessie 1105
Fiedler, Leslie A. 1133
Film scripts, "novelization" of
614-16
Fisher, Rudolph 1105, 1167

Fisk University 859
Erastus Milo Craveth Memorial
Library 864
Charles Waddell Chesnutt
Collection 832
Folk culture in fiction 901, 951
Folklore 1171
in fiction 867, 994, 1000
Ford, Nick Aaron 949, 1111
France in fiction 917
Frank, Waldo 853
French, Warren 1104
Fuller, Hoyt W. 909, 1104, 1128

## G

Gaines, Ernest J. 973, 1014-26,
1119, 1156-57
Gayle, Addison, Jr. 897
Gibson, Donald B. 883, 890, 972
Gilman, Richard 1104
Glicksberg, Charles I. 957
Gloster, Hugh M. 853
Griggs, Sutton E. 1052, 1136
Gross, Seymour L. 1133
Gross, Theodore 1104

## H

Haiku 898
Haiti in fiction 161
Harlem in fiction 287, 399, 408,
524, 782, 815
critical studies of 916, 920,
924, 929
Harlem renaissance 839, 850, 854-
55, 862-63, 1105, 1107,
1109, 1117, 1121, 1124,
1139, 1158, 1163, 1167,
1170
bibliography of 1055, 1071,
1083, 1096
Harper, Michael 1156
Hayden, Robert 1156
Hernton, Calvin C. 970
Heroes in fiction 1134
Heroines in fiction. See Women in
fiction
Himes, Chester 906-22, 923, 1152-
53, 1157

# Subject Index

Orsagh, Jacqueline 972

## P

Periodical literature, Afro-American, bibliography 1054, 1062, 1066. See also CRISIS (periodical)
Petry, Ann 907, 923-33, 1156-57, 1159
Poetry, Afro-American 788, 801, 803
  bibliography of 1095
  critical studies of 893, 1109, 1112, 1119, 1171
  See also Haiku
Publishers, black authors and 1113, 1138

## R

Realism in fiction 927, 931, 999, 1013
Record, Wilson 1104
Redding, Saunders 853, 1101, 1137
Reed, Ismael 909, 1027-38, 1128, 1156, 1164
Reilly, John M. 970, 972
Rosenfeld, Paul 853
Rovit, Earl H. 957, 959

## S

Sagas 1011
Sanders, Archie D. 950
Sanders, Ronald 897
San Francisco in fiction 409
Satire 1027, 1032-34
Schomburg Collection. See New York Public Library. Schomburg Collection of Negro Literature and History
Slave narratives 1146
  as sources for fiction 1103
Smith, William Gardner 1010, 1104
Southern states in fiction 118, 186, 294, 296, 734, 736, 753
  critical studies of 848, 852, 855, 936, 1005, 1016
  See also Alabama in fiction

South Florida, University of. Library 864
Sprandel, Katherine 898
Surrealist fiction 920
Symbolism 884, 940A, 1016, 1045

## T

Third World in fiction 983
Thurman, Wallace 1105
Toomer, Jean 847-60, 1102, 1105, 1135-36, 1164, 1166-67
Turner, Darwin T. 853, 890, 950

## V

Van Vechten, Carl 866

## W

Walker, Alice 1119, 1156-57
Warren, Robert Penn 954
Watson, Edward A. 898
Webb, Frank J. 1052
West Indies
  in fiction 748, 976, 1110
  fiction of 1120
  See also Caribbean area; Haiti in fiction
Wheatley, Phillis 1168
Wideman, John 1156
Widmer, Kingsley 1120
Williams, John A. 897, 949, 986-99, 1104, 1146, 1156, 1171
Wilner, Eleanor R. 950
Wit and humor in fiction 841, 958, 1000
  anthologies 800
Women as novelists 984
  anthologies by 827
  bibliography of 1097-98
  See also names of women novelists (e.g. Ann Petry)
World War II in fiction 382
Wright, Charles 1156
Wright, Richard 871-905A, 926, 948, 952, 955, 958, 962, 967, 987, 1062, 1071, 1074, 1102, 1118, 1123,